MARCO

CW01022751

BALTIC SEA

FINLAND
SWEDEN
Baltic
Sea
RUSSIA
DENMARK
ESTONIA
North
LATVIA
Sea
LITHUANIA
POLAND
GERMANY

Arriving on the cruise ship is already something special, because seen from the sea everything looks quite different.

Much to see, art and culture, the country and its people – a cruise offers you a multifaceted experience. And there's more: modern liners also offer you entertainment and recreation on board.

So, bon voyage and ship ahoy on your tour around the Baltic Sea!

SYMBOLS

INSIDER TIP Insider Tip

★ Highlight

↯ Scenic View

♥ Responsible travel: for ecological or fair trade aspects

PRICE CATEGORIES RESTAURANTS

Expensive over £10/US$13

Moderate £5–10/US$6–13

Budget under £5/US$6

Prices for a main dish and one non-alcoholic drink

DID YOU KNOW?
Timeline → p. 8,
Travel with kids → p. 18,
Queen Mary & Co. → p. 21,
Weather conditions → p. 27,
In the backyard → p. 30,
Rügener, Rani, Rüganer → p. 38,
Gdansk Gold Water → p. 44,
Travel with kids → p. 48,

CONTENTS

No Lithenglish, please!
→ p. 55,
Sun, sand and sea → p. 68,
Two classes at the cash
register → p. 76,
Kalevala → p. 82,
Travel with kids → p. 84,
Sweating instead of argu-
ing→ p. 87,
Island empire → p. 92,

Travel with kids → p. 95,
Silvia and Co. → p. 101,
The fascination with the elks
→ p. 102,
Round Churches → p. 111,
Child in the box → p. 120

MAPS IN THE GUIDEBOOK
(💭 1/A3) refers to the pull-
out maps

INSIDE FRONT COVER:
The best highlights

INSIDE BACK COVER:
General map

The best MARCO POLO Insider Tips

Our top 10 Insider Tips

INSIDER TIP Here's to the next round!
The *Tolsty Frajer* bar transformed Soviet agitation into ironically broken, cheerful cosiness – at absolutely fair prices → **p. 77**

INSIDER TIP Culinary art with a view of Stockholm's beauty
Where freight was once loaded via the loading hatches in the customs house, today it offers fantastic views of the old town, Skeppsholmen and Djurgården. In the café on the top floor of the photographic museum, not only visual art but also culinary art is being offered (photo below) → **p. 93**

INSIDER TIP Urban lifestyle
Due to book shops, fashion stores or bars and restaurants – in the hip waterfront area, *Långgatorna*, in Gothenburg there is a lively ambience by day and at night → **p. 103**

INSIDER TIP Small cheese wedges
Bornholm's specialties include delicious cheeses and fresh bread, which you can buy and enjoy at *Oste-Hjørnet* in Bornholm → **p. 113**

CAST OFF

DISCOVER THE BALTIC SEA!

Do you already smell the salt in the air, can you feel the wind in your hair? Yes, perhaps you also see yourself at the steering wheel of a sailing vessel like the *Hansekogge*, to trade. Above you the sails flutter in the wind, the water foams against the backdrop of the mountain. Or head out with legendary *Klaus Störtebeker* and his Victual Brothers to hijack ships. Or you set forth with a Viking ship, to conquer new worlds. Without a doubt, a glance at the *Baltic Sea* awakens fantasies of a wild, rough, yet fascinating past.

When you hear the engine noise, the humming of your modern ship will sooner or later bring you back to the present, when it casts off from the embarkation port. And perhaps you will then be very happy when you anticipate your days on the high seas, that you will be on a safe, floating hotel with all modern comforts, and not on a small, wooden cockleshell, more or less helplessly exposed to the potential challenges of the sea – but of course nobody wishes that your cruise on the Baltic Sea will be accompanied by bad weather. This ship on which you are, will now bring you out to this sea, which is also called the *Baltic Sea*, and is surrounded by countries with a rich and shared history.

Photo: On the way from the embarkation port through the Kiel Canal to the Baltic Sea

Medieval towns were part of the Hanseatic league of towns, such as *Lübeck*, *Wismar* and *Rostock* on German soil, *Stettin* and *Gdansk* in Poland or *Rīga*, the current capital of Latvia, the Estonian capital, *Tallinn* (formerly Reval). You'll definitely learn about these towns on a Baltic Sea cruise. The rich history of the Hanseatic towns is still visible toda today – all along the coast you can see magnificent brick buildings with which the Hanseatic merchants proudly showed off their wealth.

Apparently, a sea invites conquest; it did noit restrict the *Vikings* to their own shores either, and they stopped over at what is now called Schleswig-Holstein as well. Traces of the Vikings will most probably not be found in the Schleswig-Holstein capital, Kiel, but what you will definitely find is a seaside town that is charactarised by an important Baltic Sea harbour. From Kiel via the Baltic Sea, it is not far to the neighbouring country, *Denmark*, with the picturesque *Rønne* in Bornholm, or the capital, Copenhagen. A further capital, *Stockholm*, awaits you in Sweden, while the medieval *Visby* in Gotland is small but nice. Swedish

Wonderful coasts, historical cities – this is the Baltic Sea

is also spoken in the *Åland Islands* (known as the archipelago of peace due to its demilitarised status), 6,500 in total, although they actually belong to Finland. *Helsinki*, Finland's capital, should certainly also not be missed on a Baltic cruise. It's a vibrant and green city with charming architecture.

On the other side of the ocean, a dazzling pearl is waiting for you – the radiant and splendid *St. Petersburg*. The metropolis on the Neva River has something like a Fata

Around 12 000 BC – 6000 BC
End of the Ice Age. Hunter-gatherers move into the Baltic region.

100 – 600 AD
The Baltic tribes were actively trading with amber as far as the Orient

800 – 1000 AD
Viking era; Hedeby (near Schleswig) became North Europe's first trading town

1219 – 1227
The Danes built the Reval fort (now Tallinn)

1300 – 1600
Hanseatic period with flourishing Baltic trade. Visby in Gotland became one of the most important towns

Stockholm: one of many scenic destinations at the Baltic Sea

Morgana, not only for its unreal pastel lights of the famous white nights, but one just has to see the exuberant colours and forms.

The Baltic Sea region is of course much more than dreamlike towns with a long history, beautiful buildings and endless art and culture. Even nature on the Baltic coasts is unique – in the country areas there are places with nearly unspoilt forests; in the Scandinavian forests, moose and bears can still be seen. There are kilometres of sandy beaches below steep cliffs, or the thousands of islands in Finland, the *archipelago* in Sweden or Rügen's wonderful chalk cliffs that already inspired Caspar David Friedrich. It's no wonder that Unesco did not only declare towns of the Baltic Sea such as Rīga, Tallin, Visby, Lübeck and Wismar as World Heritage Sites, but also landscapes such as the *Beech Forests in Rügen*, the unique and vulnerable sand dune peninsula, *Curonian Spit* in Lithuania and Mecklenburg-Western Pomerania's *Bodden Landscape*. And what do you take home as a souvenir after a Baltic Cruise? Petrified resin sounds a bit ordinary; but beautiful amber is definitely good advice.

Late 14th c.
Störtebeker and Co. ensured Stockholm's food supply as blockade runners, as the Danish town was being sieged.

1906
Finland was the first country in Europe to introduce women's suffrage

1990
Lithuania, Latvia and Estonia declared independence from the Soviet Union

2000
Opening of the 7,845m long Öresund Bridge that connects Malmö with Copenhagen, after five years of construction

AROUND THE BALTIC SEA

RESIN FROM THE SEA

Beachcombers mostly discover the "gold of the sea" at the driftline between algae and seaweed. 300 different types of amber are known: the so-called Baltic amber is found in the Baltic Sea region, it shimmers in bright yellow to orange-red, brownish or yellowish-white. It is from the tertiary era, originating from hardened fossilised resin, which dripped from trees 40–50 million years ago and was carried to the sea by rivers.

STRONG MEN

Between 800 and 1100 AD, the Vikings from Scandinavia sailed across the sea and made a living from looting and daring trading voyages. They settled in the 9th and 10th century and founded the Schlei in Hedeby, the biggest trading centre of the north. Around 1,000 people lived here. They were sailors and pirates, traders, merchants, blacksmiths, craftsman, boat builders and carpenters who lived in houses made from reeds and wood. Today you can follow the old Viking culture in a museum that includes some reconstructed village houses at Hedeby near Schleswig.

OCEAN CONNECTION

Completed in 1895, the roughly 100 km/62 mi North-to-Baltic Sea Canal is Schleswig-Holstein's biggest and most popular landmark. It's known as the "Kiel Canal" to sailors worldwide. Yearly, around

One Ocean, ten countries: experience maritime history, various cultures and fascinating landscapes

35,000 ships pass through the waterway between Brunsbüttel and Kiel-Holtenau, cruise ships are among these. Due to the ten high bridges, their masts may not be taller than 40 m above sea level. Both locks at the beginning and end of the canal are among the biggest in the world. A fascinating spectacle is offered to onlookers at the Kiel Canal: passenger ships, huge tankers and freighters seemingly glide right through green meadows on which animals graze.

OF FLYING OBJECTS & WHISTLE BUOYS

Screaming seagulls are part of the coastal environment. They breed on the ground; the colonies often comprise thousands of pairs. One mostly sees the black-headed gull due to its identifiable red beak. The herring gull is distinguished from the common gull by the red dot on its yellow beak. Three seal species frolic in the Baltic Sea, namely the grey seal, the common seal and the ringed seal.

Truly enchanting sunrise over Rügen

EU OF MEDIEVAL TIMES

The Hanseatic League exists (again). 175 towns of the 16 European countries that already belonged to the Hanseatic League built the biggest worldwide voluntary association of towns of that time. In the medieval times, the members of the alliance of cities swore to support each other on water and on land and to ensure the economic interests of their merchants, especially abroad. The current Hanseatic League aims to revive the spirit of the collaboration of that time and to improve cooperation. Long ago the members of the powerful alliance of cities met at the Hanse convention (the last one took place in 1669) to agree to a common approach. Hanse conventions have again been held in the modern times: the new Hanseatic League was founded in 1980, and since 1990 the convention is hosted by a different city each year to celebrate and to get to know one another.

ROBIN HOOD BY SHIP

Klaus Störtebeker took from the rich and gave to the poor, so the legend went for centuries. The incredible pirate was glorified as the Robin Hood of the Baltic Sea. A total of twelve towns and villages claimed that he was from there. According to legends, he was born in Ruschvitz on the island of Rügen, another tells of a hiding place that he owned in a cave at Koserow on Usedom island. In the Baltic Sea Störtebeker and Co ensured Stockholm's food supply as blockade runners at the end of the 14th century, as the Danish town was under siege. When they were banished from the Baltic Sea, they transformed themselves into pirates and hijacked the Baltic Hanseatic cogs and English trading vessels. Soon the Hanseatic League started chasing them – with success: In 1401 Störtebeker and his companions were beheaded by the executioner in Hamburg.

LIGHT AT NIGHT

They have been indispensible for as long as anyone can remember – at least since people have been sailing the seas. Lighthouses send their light far onto the sea along the Baltic coasts to safely show ships the way. Typically, they are round, with black rings – however, exceptions prove the rule. The third oldest light tower in the world stands in Hiiumaa, already built in the 16th century and not round at all, but square and rather reminds one of a massive castle keep. Everywhere along the Baltic Sea coast one comes across the lighted beacons, mostly built from stone, sometimes also from wood or metal. Today they are controlled by sophisticated electronics. But, whoever wants to walk up the accessible platforms can just imagine what it was like when the lighthouse keepers were still there doing their duties.

VERY BEAUTIFULLY DIVERSIFIED

Anyone walking along a Baltic shore might get the impression that this beach runs all the way around this sea. But appearances are deceptive: the Baltic Sea offers a variety of coastal formations such as the archipelago in Scandinavia, with its scattering of small islands; the Pomeranian Bodden, most of which are separated from the sea; lagoons, like the Curonian lagoon at the spectacular Curonian Spit, or cliffs, of which the chalk cliffs of Rugen are an especially impressive example.

HAVE WATER, NEED BOAT

Where there's a sea, there will be boats. Ships have to be built. No wonder that there are and always have been shipbuilders on Baltic Sea.

On the Polish coast ships have been built for more than a thousand years. However, at first they were only small boats. The Pomeranians sailed to raid Denmark as early as the 9th century. In medieval times, Szczecin and Gdansk finally became shipbuilding centres that in the industrial era grew into colossal wharves – they did, however, fall victim to the market economy and the Asian competitors in the 20th century. On the other hand, Finland has one of the biggest European shipyards, where cruise ships are also built, and as before, ships are also built in Kiel.

ISLAND HOPPING IN THE NORTH

Whoever wants to can actually go island hopping – anyway, there are enough destinations, from extremely small to very big. From the tiny skerries off Sweden up to the really big islands of Zealand in Denmark, off the east coast as well as the south east coast archipelago, right up to the really thick boulders of the Danish Zealand, the largest and most populous island of Denmark, where the capital, Copenhagen, is also situated (altogether with Zealand and Funen, the Danish have hogged the biggest Baltic Sea islands), Germany's biggest island, Rügen, is connected to the mainland at Stralsund by the Rügen-damm and the Rügen-bridge, or the Estonian Saaremaa which, after Zealand, Funen and the Swedish Gotland, is the biggest island in the Baltic Sea. The Finns had to lay it on very thick because they have just about 80,000 islands. Usedom has breathtaking lakes.

GERMANY'S COASTS

No, your knowledge of geography is not letting you down: Hamburg and Bremerhaven are obviously not situated at the Baltic Sea! There are, however, some cruise providers whose tours leave from both North Sea ports, and cruises into the Baltic Sea with a direct tour along the German coasts.

Once arrived in the Baltic Sea a great variety of towns await you with evidence of a long Hanseatic past, with impressive Brick Gothic buildings on wide, often kilometre-long beaches and of course the unique white chalk cliffs of Rügen. In Kiel, not only the Schleswig-Holstein capital waits for you, but also an important harbour. Once a year, it hosts the largest sailing event of the world. Further to the east you'll explore Lübeck with the world-famous Holsten Gate, Wismar and Rostock with their historical centres and brick buildings and Germany's biggest island, Rügen with the elegant spa architecture in Sassnitz and Binz.

BREMER-HAVEN

Bremerhaven (pop. 114,000) is not part of Lower Saxony, but belongs to the two-town state, Bremen. It is the biggest town on the North Sea coast, and after Hamburg it is Germany's busiest commercial port.

History and nature: the German Baltic Sea impresses with beautiful Hanseatic towns and unique landscape

The container port and the automobile port are the most important economic pillars in Bremerhaven today, where the majority of the German automobile imports and exports are being handled. Furthermore, Bremerhaven is Germany's most important fishing harbour. The maritime orientation of the town is apparent from its university, and renowned research facilities such as the well-known Alfred Wegener Institute for Polar and Marine Research.

SIGHTSEEING

CLIMATE HOUSE 8 DEGREES EAST ★
(*1/A–B2*)
On the longitude that passes through Bremerhaven, travel adventurously to people and landscapes in all climate zones of the earth. You can walk in dry, cold weather, humid air and scorching heat – only just between the maritime museum and the emigration centre. *Apr–Aug Mo–Fri, Sa/Sun 10am–7pm, Sept–March daily 10am–6pm | 16 euros | Am*

*Längengrad 8 | Tel. 0471 9 02 03 00 |
www.klimahaus-bremerhaven.de/en*

CONTAINER LOOK-OUT-PLATFORM ☀︎

From here, at no cost, you can see how
the container harbour operates. *March–
Oct around the clock free entrance |
Parkplatz Nordschleuse*

GERMAN EMIGRATION CENTRE ★
(ᠭ 1/A2)

For the mere price of the entry ticket, you
are transformed into an emigrant, wait for
your ship in Bremerhaven, experience the
stormy transit on board and the immigra-
tion procedures on Ellis Island. Special ef-
fects and background information create
an exciting combination. In the extension
wing the theme is "First year in the new
world". *Daily 10am–5pm, March–Oct till
6pm | 12.80 euros, combination ticket
with maritime museum 16.50 euros | Co-
lumbusstr. 65 | Tel. 0471 90 22 00 | www.
dah-bremerhaven.de/english/*

GERMAN MARITIME MUSEUM ★
(ᠭ 1/B3)

Here you can see the luxury cabin of a
passenger ship from 1912 and you can
enter the midship of a side paddle
steam ship from 1881. A 1380 Hanseatic cog that sank in the Weser River
and that was salvaged in 1962, is the
museum's greatest pride. An extension is dedicated to fishery, sport-boat-
ing and whaling. The skeleton of a
sperm whale is a special attraction.
The whaler, "Rau IX", the high sea sal-
vage tug "Seefalke", the lightship
"Elbe 3" and the three-masted barque
"Seute Deern" are housed in the harbour museum. *Tue–Sun, mid-March–
Oct daily 10am–6pm, ships (except
Seute Deern) only middle March–Oct |
6 euros, combination ticket with the
Emigration Centre 16.50 euros | Hans-
Scharoun-Platz 1 | Tel. 0471 48 20 70 |
www.dsm.museum*

Maritime Museum landscape with climate house and harbour museum

HISTORICAL MUSEUM (*1/C3*)

In the modern building everything is about the history of the region and the town. Great emphasis is placed on the depiction of the living conditions and working conditions of the people. One learns a lot about fishing and fish processing, international ports, the container terminal, shipyards and ship building. *Tue–Su 10am–5pm | An der Geeste 1 | Tel. 0471 30 81 60 | www.historisches-museum-bremerhaven.de*

LOOK-OUT-PLATFORM SAIL CITY ☼ (*1/A2*)

From a height of almost 80 m/262 ft, the view over the North Sea coast and sea is spectacular! *April–Sept daily, 9am-9pm, Oct–March 10am–5pm | 3 euros | Havenwelten | Am Strom 1 | www.bremerhaven.de/en*

INSIDER TIP MUSEUM OF THE FIFTIES

The unique and very charmingly designed museum is housed in the chapel of the former US-American, Carl Schurz Barracks, in the northern part of town. Typical living environments from the 1950s, authentic in every detail, have been reconstructed: a kitchen, a petrol pump, a Bremen pub, an office, a hair salon and a doctor's practice. Fashion, design, everyday objects, and a lot more from that era of the Federal German economic miracle, can be seen in display cabinets. Informative texts were supplied by the Bremen University. *Apr–Oct Sun 11am–5pm | 5 euros | Amerikaring 9 | Tel. 0471 8 83 05 |www.museum-der-50er-jahre.de*

MUSEUM SHIP FMS GERA

This side trawler, built in Rostock in 1959/60, was laid up in the Bremerhaven fishery harbour since 1993. Until 1980, it mostly went to the North Sea to fish. *April–Oct daily 10am–6pm | 3.50 euros | Schaufenster Fischereihafen | Tel. 0471 30 81 60 | www.museumsschiff-gera.de*

NORTH SEA EXPEDITION – FISHERY WORLDS

The expedition presents the fauna of the North and Baltic Seas and the fishing tradition of the town in an entertaining way. *Daily 10am–6pm | 6 euros | Forum Fischbahnhof | Am Schaufenster 6 | Tel. 0471 3 01 00 03 | www.fischbahnhof.eu*

WILHELM BAUER U-BOAT MUSEUM ★ (*1/B2*)

A walk through the over 76m long, but only 6,60 m/22 ft width submarine U2540 from the Second World War brings to life the cramped space, the noise and the smell of oil in which the U-boat operators carried out their nightmarish missions. *Easter holidays–Oct daily 10am–6pm | 3.50 euros | Museumhafen | www.u-boot-wilhelm-bauer.de/en*

INSIDER TIP TOUR DE WIND (*1/A2*)

The two hour long almost state-wide bus drive runs from Havenwelten (Harbour Worlds) to a 190m high wind turbine testing facility, to a 500 t heavy concrete tripod like those that are submerged in the sea for the wind turbines, and to other projects associated with Bremerhaven as a centre of modern offshore wind farm technology. *March–Oct Fri from 5pm, Sat/Sun from 2:30 pm from Havenwelten opposite the Zoo | 9.90 euros, tickets from tourist info*

ZOO ON THE SEA ★ (*1/A2*)

In the small, very modern zoo, not only penguins, seals and common seals can be seen under water, but through a glass pane one can even watch polar bears dive. Chimpanzees provide the entertainment, and then there's the view of the shipping traffic in the Weser River mouth, from the café terrace. *April–Sept daily 9am–7pm, March and Oct 9am–6pm, Nov–Feb 9am–4:30pm | 8.50 euros | Hermann-Heinrich-Meier-Str. 5 | Tel. 0471 30 84 10 | zoo-am-meer-bremenhaven.de*

HAMBURG

There are days on which even die-hard Hanseatics are surprised by their city.
On a summer evening they sit with their beer on the beach by the Elbe at Övelgönne, with container ships, harbour ferries and sailing boats passing right in front of them. They take a stroll towards the city centre, past the modern developments of the Elbmeile, gaze across the water from the Dockland office block that juts out over the river and take a detour for a nightcap at the St. Pauli beach club. The stroll continues to Hafencity, where there will probably be some festival going on – jazz or literature. They might hang around for a bit and admire the imposing tinted glass façade of the Elbphilharmonie, which towers over the river. Even now, late in the evening, visitors are still strolling on the square. Mobile phone cameras flash – the view is spectacular. In the background, the new developments of the Hafencity and the illuminated façades of the Speicherstadt (warehouse district) are visible. By this stage these Hamburgers will have looked at each other and said something like: wow, we really do live in a great city!

TRAVEL WITH KIDS

HAGENBECK'S ZOO ★
One of Europe's biggest tropical aquariums with Madagascan lemurs roaming free, a sensational orangutan house, elephants that can be hand fed as well as a frozen lake that is safe to walk on that has **INSIDER TIP** walruses (the only ones in Germany!), that shake flippers with when they feed them. There are lions, tigers, bears, bisons, porcupines, mountain goats, lamas and meerkats... as well as one of the prettiest zoo areas in the world. It has been run by the Hagenbeck family for generations. *Aquarium daily 9am–6pm, zoo March–June, Sept/Oct daily 9am–6pm, July/Aug 9am– 7pm | combined ticket for park and aquarium (also available individually) 30 euros, children 21 euros | Lokstedter Grenzstr. 2 | tel. 040 5 30 03 30 | www.hagenbeck.de | U 2 Hagenbecks Tierpark*

SIGHTSEEING

RATHAUS (TOWN HALL) ★
(🕮 2/D2)
It's well worth taking a tour of the town hall: there's gold and splendour wherever you look, such as in the large Emperor's Hall, so called because it was here, on 19 June 1895, that Kaiser Wilhelm II celebrated the opening of the Kiel Canal. The great and the good of Hamburg still gather here every February, as they have done ever since 1356 to celebrate the Matthias feast along with 'representatives of those powers friendly towards Hamburg'. During the Great Fire of 1842, the old town hall near the Trost Bridge was blown up in the hope that this would help contain the blaze and prevent things getting worse. Subsequently there were decades of squabbles about a replace-

ment building. It was not until 1880, when the architect Martin Haller established the 'Town Hall Builders' Society', that there was a breakthrough. Today it is regarded as one of Germany's most important historiciststyle buildings. If your German's up to it, there are even **INSIDER TIP** guided tours in Plattdeutsch (Low German)! *tickets 4 euros | Rathausmarkt 1 | Tel. 040 4 28 31 20 64 | www.hamburg.com | U 3 Rathaus*

OLD ELBE TUNNEL *(2/A3–4)*

It rattles and shakes and is a real adventure: a descent with the car lift down (24 m/78.7 ft) to below the level of the Elbe. When the Alter Elbtunnel was built in 1911, it was an international sensation. It is 426.5 m/1399 ft long and originally served the harbour workers on their way to work. The dome on the shipping piers was modelled on the Pantheon in Rome.

The tunnel is closed to cars at weekends. *Pedestrians and cyclists round the clock and free | S-/ U-Bahn Landungsbrücken*

LANDUNGSBRÜCKEN ★ *(2/A3)*

If statistics are to be believed, the St.-Pauli-Landungsbrücken piers are – after the Brandenburg Gate in Berlin – Germany's second most visited tourist attraction. The pontoon installation was constructed between 1904–1910 and indeed, there is always nonstop bustle on the water with harbour ferries coming and going every minute and the catamaran to Helgoland or one of the two paddle steamers in between. The piers are numbered to help you find your way. The bridges are numbered to help with orientation. For example, the Hadag line ferry 62 is stationed at pier 3. Don't be put off by the commotion made by captains promoting their harbour tours,

The Landungsbrücken: just one of Hamburg's splendid sights

Hanseatic charm in the Speicherstadt

the harried commuters and day-trippers with their bikes. Buy a fish sandwich, find a place on the steps and watch the action from above. The promenade towards the city centre is new (and better protected against flooding). Stroll along here past the museum ships 'Cap San Diego' and 'Rickmer Rickmers' as far as the Hafencity. *S-/ U-Bahn Landungsbrücken*

ST. MICHAEL'S CHURCH ★ *(ω 2/B3)*

The Michaeliskirche (St. Michael's Church) – is one of the city's most important landmarks. The present magnificent baroque building was completed in 1786. After a fire completely destroyed the church in July 1906, the Senate immediately decided to reconstruct it on the same site, using the original plans. The ☀ tower is 132 m/433 ft high, and 452 steps lead to the top (there is also a lift). *Daily May–Oct 9am–7.30pm, (visits are not possible during services), combined ticket 7 euros | Englische Planke 1 | tel. 040 37 67 80 | www.st-michaelis.de | express bus 37 Michaeliskirche*

INSIDER TIP PARK FICTION

It is an exciting place, this rather offbeat little park at the edge of St. Pauli, which enjoys a fantastic view of the harbour. It was born out of a local neighbourhood action group that managed to prevail against the developers. Now, you can sip a beer or latte under artificial palm trees among punks, market researchers and children playing ball. Right next door is the once embattled port road, below at the Fischmarkt, Hamburg's cult nightclub Golden Pudel, and right opposite, the floating docks of Blohm + Voss. All of which gives the area a really special atmosphere. *Corner Antonistr./ Pinnasberg | www.park-fiction.net | S 1, 3 Reeperbahn*

WAREHOUSE DISTRICT (SPEICHERSTADT) AND HAFENCITY ★ *(ω 2/C–E,3–4)*

In order to make way for the warehouses of the ★ Speicherstadt (warehouse district) at the end of the 19th century, thousands of people were forced to leave their homes. Today the amazing ensemble of brick buildings is the jewel of the Hanseatic city. A worthwhile tip is to explore on foot and take a look at the inner courtyards at Holländische Brook and Alte Wandrahm. The warehouses look fantastic, especially in the evenings, thanks to a special lighting concept from Hamburg light artist Michael Batz. You can also explore Hafencity on foot. Get off at the Baumwall U-Bahn station (U3). From there it's just a few minutes to the Elbphilharmonie, the Kaiserkai and Lohsepark.

ELBPHILHARMONIE ★ (ᗰ 2/C4)

The ⚓ plaza is open to visitors, but at peak times (especially weekends and public holidays) it's worth booking a timed ticket in advance (2 euros, online booking is best). Then, you can take the 82-m/269-ft long and elegantly arched escalator to the upper level – and you'll probably pause for a while. The view surpasses everything that Hamburg previously had to offer. Plus, if you're one of the lucky ones who managed to acquire a concert ticket you can take a seat in the main auditorium: none of the 2,072 seats in the 16 steeply climbing rows is more than about 30 m/98.4 ft from the conductor. Connoisseurs love the (cheap) seats right at the top. The amazing sound of the Japanese acoustic specialist Yasuhisa Toyota makes this possible – a democratic way to enjoy music! *Platz der Deutschen Einheit 4 | www.elbphilharmonie.de/en | bus 111 Kaiserkai/ Elbphilharmonie*

MINIATUR-WUNDERLAND ★ (ᗰ 2/C4)

The numbers are impressive: several hundred thousand figures, more than 10 km/6.2 mi of track, tens of thousands of wagons, vehicles, etc. It is the largest model railway in the world, operated by 64 computers – and the enthusiasm of the team. The Swiss Alps alone extend over three floors; you can see the Norwegian fjords and a gigantic airport with planes taking off and landing. The best time to visit is early evening; you can **INSIDER TIP** book tickets in advance on the website and avoid the queues. *ad-*

QUEEN MARY & CO.

When the 'Queen Mary' comes to town, Hamburgers as well as tourists line the banks of the Elbe in their thousands. They wave and jostle around, there is special coverage of the event on television, bakers bake bread rolls in the shape of a ship: it's party time on the Elbe. The number of cruise ships arriving in Hamburg increases year on year. The *Cruise Days* have become a huge event. The biggest and most beautiful cruise ships visit Hamburg every September. At night, they cruise down the Elbe, bathed – like half the port and other parts of the city – in a mysterious blue light: The **INSIDER TIP** *Blue Port* is a creation of light artist and theatre maker Michael Batz. Meanwhile, there are various cruise terminals between Altona and Steinwerder, and building works are ongoing at Hafencity.

mission 12 euros | Kehrwieder 2 | tel. 040 3 00 68 00 | www.miniatur-wunderland. com | metro bus 6 Auf dem Sande

INSIDER TIP ERNST BARLACH HOUSE

This may be one of the nicest little museums in Hamburg. Werner Kallmorgen's modest building in the centre of Jenisch-Park is noteworthy for its clean lines. It now houses the magnificent collection of the Hamburg patron (and former tobacco magnate) Hermann F. Reemtsma. The sculptor Ernst Barlach was ostracised and persecuted by the Nazis but Reemtsma was undeterred and continued to give him commissions. *Tue–Sun 11am–6pm | admission 6 euros | Baron-Voght-Str. 50 a | tel. 040 82 60 85 | www.ernst-barlach-haus.de/en | metro bus 15 Marxenweg*

FISCHMARKT/FISCHAUKTIONSHALLE (FISH MARKET)

It is a ritual end to a party or pub crawl in Hamburg to visit the Fischmarkt (fish market). It's a very entertaining experience with lots of colourful characters; the banter employed by the fruit and fish sellers may not be the politest but they put on a great show, and even by 6am there's usually a huge throng of visitors. Besides fish and seafood there are stalls selling fruit and vegetables, and the pot plants for 5 euros make a nice souvenir *(Sun, April–Oct 5am–9.30am, Nov–March 7am–9.30am). Bus 111 Fischauktionshalle*

GROSSE ELBSTRASSE (STREET)

It has been quite a while now, since this street was notorious for kerb crawling. Today it's lined not by prostitutes and their clients but by one new building after another. The PR people call it a 'pearl necklace on the Elbe', though many of the 'pearls' remain empty. It's the same old story: glass, concrete and astronomical rents. Nevertheless a walk from the fish market to Övelgönne is interesting and there are a number of nice restaurants. Designed by architect Hadi Teherani, the ⚲ INSIDER TIP *Dockland* is a spectacular office building shaped like a ship. You can climb the 140 steps onto the 'bridge' – the roof – where you'll be rewarded with sensational views. *S 1, 3 Königstraße | bus 111 Große Elbstraße*

INSIDER TIP OTTENSEN

This was always (and will hopefully long remain) Hamburg's liveliest district. The colourful mélange is unique in the city. Punks and pensioners, yuppies and ecowarriors, creatives and promoters – everyone lives here peacefully side by side. In Ottensen you can find some of the city's nicest restaurants, as well as unusual shops, delicatessens, cafés, fashion boutiques, pubs, Turkish snack stalls and trendy bars. For decades all attempts by estate agents and the property developers to harmonise the attractive hotchpotch by putting up boring new buildings have failed. *Bus and S-Bahn Altona*

Blankenese: a prestigious district

SHOPPING

A sailor shirt or a designer gown? Hamburg is a shopper's paradise

Shopping in Hamburg is a lot of fun, whether in the heart of the city or in the lively surrounding districts.
All around the Jungfernstieg and the Gänsemarkt, in the Hanseviertel and the Hamburger Hof you'll find exclusive haute couture and jewellery shops. Department stores and cheaper shops are located towards the Hauptbahnhof. And small, quality shops you will find along the city's side streets, e.g. around Poolstraße near the Laieszhalle, where bespoke tailors and young designers offer their wares for sale. There are numerous shops along the exclusive Eppendorfer Baum and the Lange Reihe in St. Georg, where window-shopping is a lot of fun. In Ottensen, in the Schanzenviertel and in Winterhude there is an unbelievable variety of fashion boutiques, delicatessens and specialist outlets. The top address for fashion 'made in Hamburg', vinyl records and quirky artisan shops like Lockengelöt is the Karolinenviertel (Karoviertel for short) and Marktstraße. In the city centre shops are usually open until 8pm, smaller shops may close earlier. On the Reeperbahn shopping can also be done at night.

SHOPPING ARCADES

Theoretically you could shop all day between Gänsemarkt and Hauptbahnhof (main railway station) without feeling a single drop of rain. The Europa-Passage, designed by Hamburg's favourite architect Hadi Teherani, is the largest shopping mall in the city. It is a five-storey palace of consumerism (from the top you have a superb view over the Binnenalster) with glass lifts, shops, fast food outlets and even an art gallery displaying works by Germany's aging rocker Udo Lindenberg. Whether for people watching or more exclusive shopping, the locals also like going to *Galleria*, where a French bistro serves café au lait or champagne to go with the view over the canal. Architects also succeeded in converting the *Levantehaus*, a 100-year-old Kontorhaus office building on Mönckebergstraße, into a chic shopping arcade with small outlets.

ÖVELGÖNNE ⭐

The picturesque row of old captains' and ship pilots' houses on the banks of the Elbe is only a few hundred metres long. Don't miss a visit to the nowadays almost famous Strandperle *(Övelgönne 60 | daily in summer, Sat/Sun in winter and depending on the weather)*, a great beach bar right on the Elbe: feet in the sand, glass in your hand, watching the ships (and of course people) go by. You will find wonderful old ships in the Museumshafen Övelgönne *(free admission | www.museumshafen-oevelgoenne)*. Under the glass dome on the roof of the Augustinum old age home is 🔆 *Café Elbwarte* (Wed and Sat/ Sun 3–6pm). The view is well worth it. *Bus 112 Neumühlen*

KIEL

Up until 140 years ago, Kiel was a relatively small university town. It only started growing after emperor Wilhelm II declared it an Imperial War Harbour in 1872. With the building of the Kiel canal, the fjord town became part of international shipping. In the second World War, the town with its seven century old centre was almost totally destroyed. Today, Kiel (246,000 pop.) is the political and cultural centre of Schleswig-Holstein, a ferry and freight harbour, an industrial and shipbuilding hub and home of the navy.

In the summer, cruise ships arrive at Kiel. Pedestrians have the best view of the harbour activity along the Kiellinie. Around the castle garden, the eight seaside museums *(www.museum-am-meer.de)* beckon, which cover all interests from art about town and maritime history to zoology. Crossing the Hörn bridge, a folding pedestrian bridge at the end of the fjord, you reach the east bank and stroll to the classic sailing boats in the Germania harbour and along Willy-Brandt-shore.

GEOMAR AQUARIUM *(📖 3/D1)*

A window into the North and Baltic Seas, into exotic underwater worlds and an outdoor seal pool. The *public feedings (Sat–Thu 10am and 2:30pm)* are a popular spectacle. *Daily 9am–6pm | Admission 3 euros | Düsternbrooker Weg 20*

GORCH FOCK

When the Gorch Fock is not sailing on the world's oceans, it is at the Tirpitz harbour. The 81m long, snow white three-masted barque, was employed as the Federal Navy sail training ship in 1958. Officers and NCO candidates start their careers here. During Kiel week, the windjammer is often seen sailing.

KIEL ART MUSEUM *(📖 3/D1)*

International and Scandinavian art of the 19th and 20th centuries forms the main focus of the collection of Kiel's biggest museum, but contemporary art is also presented. The antique collection department on the ground floor collects copies true to the original, of famous antique sculptures. *Thu–Sun 10am–6pm, Wed till 8pm | Admission 7 euros | Düsternbrooker Weg 1*

OLD MARKET *(📖 3/C2)*

At the northern end of Holsten Street, Germany's first pedestrian zone, is the old market. The square with the St. Nikolai Church marks the historic centre of the town that was ruined during the Second World War.

RATHAUS (TOWN HALL) *(📖 3/C2)*

The spacious constructed facility in art nouveau style, is overlooked by the 106m high town hall tower, Kiel's landmark. There is a stunning view from the viewing gallery – which is closed for renovations for the time being.

LOCKS ⭐

It is perceived precision work when the ships thread through the locks of the Kiel canal. The best view is from the ☀ *Look-out platform (sunrise till sunset | Admission 1 euro)* in the southern part of town, Wik. Around 30,000 ships pass through today's busiest manmade waterway in the world, reopened since 1895. From the camper site ☀ *kiosk*, from the outdoor seats, one also has an awesome view of the action at the Fjord and canal. A bit further away, you are at the ☀ *Wik balcony*, the 2.30m high observation deck in *Schleusenpark*. Since you are already there, you should trudge around the 27 other locations of the *Culture Mile (www.maritimes-viertel.*

de), which runs through the Wik and Holtenau districts. You reach Holtenau on the northern side of the canal by passenger ferry or by crossing the high bridge. An excursion to the Holtenau Lighthouse is recommended. Here, in the ☀ *Luzifer im Fördeblick (daily | Kanalstr. 85 | Tel. 0431 32 09 74 24 | www. foerdeblick-kiel.de | Budget–Moderate)* you can watch the ships from the terrace behind panoramic windows in the winter, or from the rustic *Schiffercafé (daily | Tiessenkai 9 | www.schiffercafe-kiel.de)* one can look at ships.

TOWN AND MARITIME MUSEUM
(🗺 3/D2)

The maritime history of the town is presented in two historical exhibition buildings, the impressive *Fish Auction Hall* at the harbour, from 1910 and in the 400 year old *Warleberger Hof (Dänische*

A Kiel institution: the sail training ship, Gorch Fock

Str.19), at the Old Market. In the summer semester, there an additional floating department at the *museum bridge*, behind the *Fish Auction Hall*, where three classic ships can be viewed. *Thu–Sun 10am–6pm, Thu till 8pm | Free entrance*

SHOPPING

The classy shopping centre with levels is the glass covered ⭐ *Sophienhof,* with two retail levels. *The Holtenau Arcades* in Holtenauer Street and the pedestrian zone in *Holsten and Dänische Streets*, are also popular shopping areas.

FLENSBURG

Beate Uhse, the traffic sinner card file, or beer that goes pop: These are the things that come to mind to German people who visit ⭐ Flensburg for the first time.

The northernmost town of Germany, with its 94,000 inhabitants and a stone's throw away from Denmark, is anything

but boring. With 700 years of trading and harbour commerce, and the use of the Danish krone for 400 of these years – the town has left its mark. Earlier, even the most powerful merchant fleets sailed from here. Today one can stroll through hidden courtyards and past old merchant houses with Danish composure and drink a cocktail at the Hafenspitze (harbour tip). And whoever thought that the north is generally flat should walk up Museum Hill. The young-at-heart university town with its international residents is charming even when it rains. Then one simply goes to one of the rum distilleries. Would you like to swim? Please: with its length of 34 km/21 mi, the Flensburg Fjord offers many possibilities.

SIGHTSEEING

FLENSBURG BREWERY (🗺 4/C4)

Have you always wanted to learn the origin of the "beer that goes pop"? The tour of the Flens brewery starts with the brewhouse up to the bottling plant takes around three hours. Afterwards there is

Historical shop at the Flensburg Harbour Museum

WEATHER CONDITIONS

A sign of a storm is when the sheep have no more locks, it is raining when the herrings swim past at eye level. Everything under wind force 12 is a light breeze. There are many sayings about North German weather. There is also no other place where the sky is so beautifully grey as in the north when the wind blows over thick pewter-coloured clouds. Some years April lasts until the end of September, then seamlessly changes into autumn. Snow is therefore rather rare. In the summer, the sun is out and makes the ocean shine azure blue, and the fields lush green, then an almost Mediterranean lightness is in the air. Don't you wonder about the hardened people who lie on the beach in their bikinis when the air temperature is 17 degrees, and jump into the 15 degree warm Baltic Sea. They are definitely locals. Then they also don't say anything when holiday goers rather walk around in fleece and long pants. There is ultimately no bad weather, only wrong clothing.

a snack and one may taste. What? Flens, of course. *Mon–Fri 10am, 2pm and 6pm, May–Sept also Sat | Entrance 9.50 euros, at 6pm 12.50 euros | Munketoft 12 | Nähe hbf. | Anmeldung Tel. 0461 86 31 22 | www.flens.de*

FLENSBURG MUSEUM HILL ☆ (*⑪ 4/B3*)

Is old furniture or contemporary art your thing? Then you should take a walk up Museum Hill and immerse yourself in expressionist painting or modern art in between farmhouse rooms. Enjoy the absolutely most beautiful view over the fjord. *Thu–Sun 10am–5pm, May–Sept Thu till 8pm | Entrance 6 euros | Museumsberg 1 | www.museumsberg-flensburg.de*

HARBOUR MUSEUM (*⑪ 4/B1*)

When the wind sweeps through the mast forest in the harbour museum, the 30 traditional ships start moving. The *Alexandra* is also housed there (Tel. 0461 18 29 18 05 | *www.dampfer-alexandra.de*). It is taxing work for the stoker of the saloon steamboat: he works on the last seaworthy coal-fired ship in the country. ★ *Fjord round trips and special trips from May till Sept. from www.museumshafen-flensburg.de*

MARITIME MUSEUM ★ (*⑪ 4/B2*)

What would the seamen have been without their rum? That is probably what the museum founders of the historical customs building thought. While everything above reflects the maritime history of the town, it still smells like rum in the cellar. Earlier, big oak barrels with the sailors' favourite brew were stored here. Today the space houses the *rum museum.* The *museum yard* is situated outside the door, where historical ships are still being restored and recreated. Here, trainee boat builders learn how to use traditional tools. *Tue–Sun 10am–5pm |Entrance 6 euros | Schiffbrücke 39 | www.schiffahrts-museum.flensburg.de*

NORDERSTRASSE – GROSSE STRASSE (STREET) PEDESTRIAN ZONE – HOLM (*⑪ 4/B2–C3*)

Would you like to be practical? In Flens-

LOW BUDGET

The Flensburg *Kapitänsweg* informs about the Flensburg sailor history and everyday life in the 19th century at no charge, by means of illustrated pictures. The 5 km/3 mi long tour goes around the Hafenspitze (starts at the maritime museum).

burg you can combine shopping and sightseeing. Most of the attractions are between Südermarkt and Nordertor. So you can for example take a look at the *Old Flensburg House (Norderstr. 8)*, and admire the organ at *St. Nikolai* at Südermarkt, and then disappear into the next shop. You are also allowed to walk through unknown gates, as they may lead to well-restored merchant houses. Don't feel like researching? Simply ask *tourist info.*

The venerable St. Mary's Church

NORDERSTRASSE *(ΩΩ 4/B2)*
Hundreds of shoes dangle from the ropes across the street. Apparently they come from shoe buyers that dispose of their old trainers in this way. Now it is art 2.0.

NORDERTOR *(ΩΩ 4/B1)*
The stepped gable, constructed in 1595, is the landmark of the town. Above the archway there is a town- and a royal Danish coat of arms. There is an exhibition about the Flensburg aeronaut, Hugo Eckener (1868-1954).

PHÄNOMENTA ★ *(ΩΩ 4/B1)*
Just don't touch anything? Science is silly? But not at Phänomenta. There you are free to press buttons at 200 stations, operate switches and pull levers. Additionally, you also learn something. A wow physics experience is guaranteed. *Tue–Fri 10am–6pm, Sat/Sun 12pm–6pm | Entrance 11 euros | Norderstr. 157–163 | www.phaenomenta-flensburg.de*

ST. MARY'S CHURCH *(ΩΩ 4/B2)*
The three-nave church is almost as old as the town, the foundations were laid in 1284. Also have a look at the altar and the ceiling frescos, which also display secular scenes, e.g. the "Wild Man" slaying a bear.

SHOPPING

Renovated *merchant courtyards* with boutiques, antiques and shopping centres branch from the pedestrian zone. The *Flensburg Gallery* for example, offers over 70 shops. The *Rote Straße* (Red Street) is a centre for artists. Wednesdays and Saturdays there are weekly markets (7am–1pm) at *Südermarkt.*

FOOD & DRINK

From traditional to "fine local cuisine": at the coast people don't just prefer hearty meals

Food and drink keep body and soul together." This much quoted phrase is fondly characteristic of the Schleswig-Holstein locals. The regional cuisine in the north of the country is very hearty and for tourists it is also a culinary area of new discoveries.

Fresh Baltic fish is at the top of the menu, but meat dishes and soups are not despised by the Schleswig-Holstein inhabitants.

Many gastronomes have newly discovered the regional cuisine and serve traditional dishes in a contemporary way. For dishes with fresh ingredients that are produced locally, the *initiative "fine local"*, is advertised by chefs, producers and visitors that have merged (restaurants and recipes at *www.feinheimisch.de*) "Fine local" cuisine has now acquired quite some status. The Schleswig-Holstein Gourmet Festival is a flagship that attracts *top chefs* to the country from September to March (*www.gourmetfestival.de*).

The long-established alternative is the *Ostseegericht.* For 30 years culinary establishments at the coast and inland have been competing at the start of the season, to make the most original and tastiest dishes, which are then always offered a favourable fixed price during a season. Meat from robust cattle that live at Schleswig-Holstein's foundation for Nature Conservation and that are "landscapers" on the foundation's property, is mainly being used in the north of the country and is available on tables at selected restaurants from July till October (Info and addresses on *www. sh-geniesserland.de*).

And did you know that there is a cheese street at the Baltic Sea *(www. kaesestrasse-sh.de)*, along which selected farms sell cows', goats' and sheep's milk products? A peculiarity that the more daring visitor might want to try out: The locals sprinkle sugar on almost everything, even on kale.

BEACH

Instead of sightseeing, what about feeling the sand between your toes? Simply get onto the bus line 3 and go to the main beach in Flensburg, *Solitüde*. Here it is about fine sand in shallow water, watched by the German Lifeguard Association during peak season. Or go towards the western Fjord, to the smaller beach sections, *Ostseebad* and *Wassersleben*.

LÜBECK

The question is: what should one see first in Lübeck ⭐ (pop. 220,000)? After all, the town is the "Queen of the Hanseatic League" and is a World Heritage site.

Narrow streets? There are plenty, as are passageways with small houses, superb churches and almost everything is made from brick. The few

IN THE BACKYARD

You can discover a parallel world behind the merchant houses. Slip through narrow passages, but don't press your nose against the windows of the small guest houses – they are inhabited. Simple people used to live here 700 years ago. Those days the town burst at the seams and led the merchants to make passages in front of the rows of houses, and shacks in their gardens. Until 40 years ago, only those who had to, lived there. Today there are still a few.

architectural blunders are immaterial. They arose after the 1942 airstrike that destroyed a fifth of the town, and the gaps have to be filled.

SIGHTSEEING

MUSEUM BEHNHAUS DRÄGERHAUS (𝄞 5/B2)

Paintings, paintings and paintings: Paul Klee, Edvard Munch, Emil Nolde. Lyonel Feininger and other renowned artists of the 19th and 20th centuries hang here. That can become boring? Definitely not besides the pictures, the building is also eye-catching. *April–Dec Tue–Sun 10am–5pm | Entrance 7 euros | Königstr. 9–11 | museum-behnhaus-draegerhaus.de*

BUDDENBROOKS HOUSE (𝄞 5/B2)

Have you ever walked around on the setting of a novel? Thomas Mann created a literary monument of his family with his novel "Buddenbrooks", which is brought to life in the 1758 Buddenbrooks House. *April–Dec daily 10am–6pm | Entrance 7 euros | Mengstr. 4 | www.buddenbrookhaus.de*

EUROPEAN HANSEMUSEUM ⭐ (𝄞 5/B1)

Back into the past! You can practically smell it, spices and colourful material that previously hung at the Bruges textile market. Only when you go through the hall you realise that the scene belongs to the European Hansemuseum. It portrays 600 years of history of the most powerful economic alliance of the medieval times, by means of reconstructed scenes and original objects. It is so realistic that one almost believes to be in the middle of it. *Daily 10am–6pm | Entrance 11.50 euros | An der Untertrave 1 | www.hansemuseum.eu/language/en*

It once featured on the 50 DM: the Holsten Gate

GÜNTER-GRASS-HAUS (🗺 5/C2)

His books and thoughts, his paintings and graphic works: Grass spent a lot of time in his house. Even though the winner of the Nobel Prize for Literature passed away in 2015, his presence is still perceptible. *April–Dec daily 10am–5pm | Entrance 7 euros | Glockengießerstr. 21 | www.guenter-grass-haus.de*

HOSPITAL OF THE HOLY SPIRIT (🗺 5/B2)

A bed and a chest of drawers: there was not much space in the cubby-holes of the medieval retirement home. Seniors incidentally still live here, but in the extension. Today the 1280 building with its five towers, that partly operate as a church and a hospital, is being used for events. *Tue–Sun 10am–5pm | Entrance free | Koberg 11*

HOLSTEN GATE (🗺 5/B2)

Do you have the feeling that the landmark is askew? Yes, it is. Go in regardless and learn about the history of the town. Despite the tilt, it will certainly last another 700 years. *April–Dec daily 10am–6pm | Entrance 7 euros | Holstentorplatz*

AT THE UPPER TRAVE (🗺 5/B3)

Max takes the violin and bow, closes his eyes and plays. Liszt, then Brahms. The first people already stand still and listen. Where is one ever offered a free concert? Not so seldom at all at the upper Trave, here is the Academy of Music, and therefore many people move their rehearsals outside. The short 800m long promenade along the Trave river is Lübeck's unofficial meeting place, where Lübeck locals and tourists mingle. It is definitely not Paris, but there is a lot of strolling here too. A few metres further, at the tables at pubs and restaurants, you'll find locals out for an after-work beer or dancing tango or salsa. The further you walk along the street, the narrower it gets. Then the promenade disappears and it becomes a grass strip with fluttering washing on the line and residents in deck chairs in front of their doors. Summer in the town.

Lübeck's old town is a Hanseatic dream

TOWN HALL *(🚲 5/B2)*

Something that takes long will eventually be completed. The Lübeck citizens pottered about on the Town Hall for nearly 300 years and incorporated stylistic elements from Gothic to Renaissance. As "Queen of the Hanseatic League" they wanted to flaunt. Go in quietly and go on a guided tour. Perhaps you will meet the mayor. *Mon–Fri 11am, noon, 3pm, Sa/Sun 1:30pm | Tour 4 euros.*

ST. MARY'S CHURCH *(🚲 5/B2)*

For structural engineers it is almost a miracle that the St. Mary's Church is still standing, because the 38m high vault was an experiment. You can incidentally admire it from the top while on a tour. Absolutely also have a look at the mechanical organ, which is one of the world's largest. *April–Sept daily 10am–6pm, Oct 10am–5pm | Entrance 3 euros*

ST. PETER'S CHURCH ⚜️ *(🚲 5/B2)*

At 50m, you are at eye level with the seagulls on the *viewing platform (elevator March–Sept daily 9am–8pm) | Admisison 3.80 euros).* **INSIDER TIP** Events often take place in the church. *www.st-petri-luebeck.de*

WILLY BRANDT HOUSE *(🚲 5/B2)*

Did you know that Willy Brandt was a Lübeck citizen? Learn more about the politician and Nobel Prize winner here. *Daily 11am–6pm | Entrance free | Königstr. 21 | www.willy-brandt.de/house-luebeck*

SHOPPING

Shopping cravings can be satisfied in the pedestrian zone of *Breiten Street*, where the *Niederegger Café* is also situated. There are more shops around the *Kohlmarkt* as well as in *König Street*. Hold onto your money in the boutiques, bars and cafés in INSIDERTIP Hüx, Glockengießer and Fleischhauer Streets.

TRAVE-MÜNDE

⭐ **Travemünde (pop. 13,500) is in Lübeck and has a long tradition as a seaside resort.**

In 1800 people already "relaxed" on the Travemünde beach. Today the old spa house houses the Wellness Hotel, *A-ROSA (www.a-rosa.de)* with gourmet restaurant. Today the casino, once well known throughout Europe, is a luxurious hotel *(Atlantic Grand Hotel | short.travel/osh13)*. There is a lively bustle at the car-free Vorderreihe with cafés, restaurants and shops. A Danish-style town is situated on the peninsula opposite, *Priwall* (ferry connection). During Travemünde week in July, you will meet many sailing enthusiasts.

SIGHTSEEING

OLD LIGHTHOUSE ☼

It is 142 steps high, you'll manage it. The view from one of Germany's oldest preserved lighthouses, which there is now a maritime museum, is super. *July/Aug daily 11am–4pm, April–Oct, Tue–Sun 1pm–4pm | Entrance 2 euros | www.leuchtturm-travemuende.de*

BRODTEN STEEP BANK ☼

At the end of the beach promenade a steep coastal part starts, that increasingly falls victim to breakers. A beautiful walk leads to Niendorf, stop at Hermannshöhe for a coffee break *(daily | www.die-hermannshoehe.de | Budget)*.

INSIDERTIP PRIWALL BALTIC STATION ☼

What lives out there in the harbour basin? And how did it develop? Answers to these questions can be found at the brand-new designed Baltic Station. *April–Oct, Tue–Sun 9am–6pm | Entrance 7 euros, with tour 9 euros | Am Priwallhafen 10 | ostseestation-priwall.de*

FOUR-MASTED BARQUE PASSAT

The landmark of Travemünde, the Passat, is situated at Priwall. Below deck, the 1911 four-masted barque, which was built in Hamburg, informs about the eventful history with an exhibition.

INSIDERTIP SEASIDE RESORT MUSEUM

How people once relaxed in Travemünde is being documented in an exhibition in the community house at the *St. Lawrence Church*. When you are already there, take a look at the wooden ceiling and the baroque altar of the church. It is worth it. *March–Dec Tue–Sun 11am–5pm | Entrance 5 euros | Torstr. 1*

WISMAR

This is the town of the stiff neck. Wismar's medieval facades and church towers are so captivatingly beautiful that you can't stop looking up.

Wismar (pop. 42,000) offers and Stralsund are neck-and-neck for the most beautiful old town. Since 2002, both towns have World Heritage Status. All the medieval and classical residential houses in the streets and alleys around the market place and harbour with the Water Gate and the Hanseatic cog creates an atmospherically dense scene for a walk around town. The town has been a member of the Hanseatic League from the 13th century, was part of Sweden for a long time, had an efficient shipyard during the GDR era and scores points with tourists today.

SIGHTSEEING

CHURCHES

All four are from brick, they are all different. Of the *St. Mary's Church (April–Sept daily 9am–5pm tower ascent until one hour before closing time | Entrance free, tour 3 euros)* it is just the tower that still stands, the *Church of the Holy Spirit (May–Sept daily 10am–6pm | Tours upon request: Tel 03841 28 35 28)* has beautiful ceiling frescos, the *Church of St. Nicholas (May–Sept daily 10am–8pm | Tours by arrangement via mail; wismar-nikolai@elkm.de)* is the giant that overtops them all. And the recently constructed *St. George's Church* functions as a stage for concerts and theatre performances. The viewing platform *(April–Sept daily 9am–5pm) | Entrance 3 euros | St.-Gerogen Kirchhof 1 A)* can also be reached with an elevator.

MARKET SQUARE ★ *(6/C3)*

The *waterworks*, built in Dutch Renaissance style, was supposed to ensure the water supply of the town. But this never happened, instead, it is the landmark of the town. The gleaming white classic town hall is also situated at the market. No more judgements are being passed at the *court house (10am–5pm | Entrance free)*, but exhibitions are held there.

OLD HARBOUR ★ *(6/B2)*

At the old harbour, warehouse buildings and the *Treehouse (April–Oct daily 9am–5pm, Nov–March 10am–4pm | Entrance free)* are reminders of the times when the harbour was a trading centre for goods. It is still one today on Sundays, when it is a fish market. From the Treehouse, where you can see art exhibitions, to the other side the harbour was closed off with a chain. And that is where the house got its name; Baum means both "tree" and "boom" (barrier). Today replicas of the two Swedish heads stand in front of the Treehouse. And the originals? It can be seen in the Schabbellhaus. When you walk around the technology centre, catch a beautiful glimpse from the quay edge of Wendorf and the beach.

POEL COG *(6/B1)*

With a trip on the Wissemara you will feel like a Hanseatic merchant at the start of an uncertain business journey while standing on board, because the ship is a replica of a cog from the 14th century. *Visit by prior arrangement, May–Oct regular trips | Entrance free | in the old harbour | Tel. 03841 30 43 10 | www.poeler-kogge.de*

SCHABBELLHAUS *(6/C2)*

The creepiest exhibition pieces of the museum are two mummified hands that were removed from a murder victim of the Middle Ages, to be buried with the murderer as part of the enforced sentence. But the Schabbellhaus (the Renaissance building itself is certainly worthy of an exhibition) also displays harmless objects about the town history. *Tue–Sun 10am-6pm, July, Aug also Mon | Entrance 8 euros | Schweinsbrücke 8 | www.schabbellhaus.de*

ROSTOCK

Ta-da! Rostock (pop. 206,000) is the only major city in Mecklenburg-Western Pomerania, with everything that comes with it: cruise ship harbour, airport, university, arts and culture scene.

The sleepy atmosphere which, despite undeniable beauty, pervades many of the smaller coastal towns, is quickly being blown out of Rostock's streets by the Baltic wind. Therefore you need to thoroughly make use of going out, eating out and celebrating, for example in the Kröpeliner Tor suburb where it actually sometimes feels like being in a neighbourhood prison.

SIGHTSEEING

MONASTERY GARDEN AND CULTURAL HISTORY MUSEUM (𝕞 7/B3)

Breathe deeply! In the evenings concerts mostly take place in the *monastery garden*, which is not far from the city centre. Within the *Cultural History Museum (Tue–Sun 10am–6pm | Entrance free | Kloster-hof 7 | www.kulturhistorisches-museum-rostock.de/en/museum)* walls you can see pieces from the artistic and cultural history of the town, such as coins or toys, but also an exhibition of the so-called degenerate art from the National Socialism period.

ST. MARY'S CHURCH (𝕞 7/C2)

Definitely go in: pulpit, altars, organ and baptismal font are all worth a look. But the ★ astronomical clock gives one goosebumps. It is from 1472, shows days, moon phases and sunrise times, chimes are played every hour, and it still works (a new calendar disc was installed with the 800-year city anniversary). INSIDER TIP ▶ The best visiting time: noon. A door opens and six apostle figures walk past Jesus, who raises His hand to bless them. *www.marienkirche-rostock.de*

NEW MARKET (𝕞 7/C2)

Market sellers spread out their goods daily in front of coloured, gabled houses in blended styles. The magnificent building on the square is the *town hall (Mon–*

Around the New Market in Rostock there are rows of historical houses

Warnemünde's landmark, the "teapot" and the lighthouse

Fri 8am–4pm), behind its baroque façade, there is a gothic nucleus. It is best to have a look inside and at the bricks, to get an impression of the age of the building (700 years!).

ST. PETER'S CHURCH ⚲ (*ᗰ 7/D2*)

An elevator takes you to the 45m high platform of the tower *(entrance 3 euros)*. The climb up the stairs is more beautiful and sportier. With Mr. Wegener *(mobile 0162 1 71 06 40)*, you can arrange `INSIDER TIP` a walk up forgotten spiral staircases and to the roof. The church (14th century) itself has a few beautiful details, e.g. the door handles by sculptor Jo Jastram that portray Adam and Eve. *www.petrikirche-rostock.de*

SHOPPING

ARTQUARIUM

Art in the form of ice buckets, maritime graffiti and lovely clothes... "producer gallery", is what artists call this house, from where they exhibit and sell artwork, through which they mutually support each other and find a bigger market (perhaps you too?). *Closed on Mon. | Barnstorfer Weg 36 | www.artquarium-rostock.de*

RONJAESPRESSO

The shop right on the Doberaner Platz (square) is tiny. Once can of course have a quick roasted coffee here, before you discover supplies for your house. *Doberaner Str. 158 | www.ronjaespresso.de*

WARNE-MÜNDE

Warnemünde (pop. 6,700) is a pretty seaside resort at the Warnow River mouth, and is full of holidaymakers in the summer. It is also Germany's biggest cruise ship harbour and an important ferry terminal, a shipyard and an institute for Baltic Sea Research. The close proximity to the big city Rostock and the very lively harbour is like vitality shot. At ★ *Alten Strom*, the promenade, shops, cafés and restaurants await visitors, while ridiculously high cruise ships slide past historical houses, cranes. The lighthouse and the "teapot", a prestigious GDR building on the promenade, characterise the skyline of Warnemünde.

SIGHTSEEING

WARNEMÜNDE LIGHTHOUSE ☀

Up until the second balcony of the 1898 tower, there are 137 stairs. Due to the far-reaching view over Warnemünde and the Baltic Sea, it is worth your while to undertake this.

WARNEMÜNDE LOCAL HISTORY MUSEUM

You can take a look at the bedrooms and living rooms of Warnemünde families at the turn of the previous century, with costumes and souvenirs of helmsmen and captains; you can get a rough idea of how life was in this coastal area back then. *Apr–Oct Tue–Sun | Entrance 3 euros | Alexandrinenstr. 31 | www.heimatmuseum-warnemuende.de*

SASSNITZ/ RÜGEN

Here people still work hard: in Sassnitz (pop. 9,400), the second biggest town in Rügen. Fishermen and employees of the nearby Mukran ferry harbour, live here.

In the GDR, the labour town was grey, but now Sassnitz reveals its old splendour. White mansions in resort architecture, a vibrant harbour to explore and an elegant curved steel suspension bridge, over which you can stroll from the centre to the Baltic Sea: Sassnitz is back, modern and elegant at the same time.

BUTTERFLY PARK

What is landing on your shoulder? The butterflies in the tropical house at the Butterfly Park are not afraid of contact. Over 140 different species flutter here through the area, a vibrant sea of colours. *April–Oct daily 10am–5pm | Straße der Jugend 6 | www.schmetterlingspark-sassnitz.de*

INSIDER TIP DWASIEDEN

In the former castle park you will find remains of completely different periods. There are the marble pillars and tiled floors that belonged in a castle, which was built from aristocratic funds from the era of Bismarck. Later it was blown up by the Red Army, but the overgrown ruins are still there. It is in the same park as the Great Dolmen, close to the Hochuferweg in the national park, and with its 35m length and two eye-catching guardian stones, it can't be overlooked. In the remaining 100 ha park area, nature offers a wonderful place for a picnic. *Schlossallee*

FISH AND HARBOUR MUSEUM

The "Havel", a 26m long fishing boat, is the star of the museum in the heart of the town harbour. In the exhibition you will learn how the "King's route" to Trelleborg came about. Or why Honecker planned the Mukran ferry harbour in secret. Exciting! *April–Oct daily 10am–5pm | at the town harbour | www.hafenmuseum.de*

U-BOAT MUSEUM

Do you still remember the poor sailors in "The Boat"? This spooky corridor hall, the painful narrowness, the heat when diving? You can try on the *H.M.S Otus,* a 90m long British a U-boat sailor, to see if you have the makings of the U-boat sailors. *Daily summer holiday 10am–7pm or May–Oct 10am–6pm, Nov–April 10am–4pm | at the town harbour | www.hms-otus.com*

SHOPPING

How about a soap cake? Or rather a bath bomb? Just like the other soap that the 🌀 *Inselseifen (Hauptstr. 10 | www.inselseifen.de)* team sells, it is made from natural products such as Rügen's healing chalk, sea buckthorn oil or berries – by hand! At the demonstration workshop you can also look over the shoulders of the soap makers while they do their work. Neat! At the town harbour you can obtain all the products of the island at *Rügenmarkt (Hafenstr. 12d | short.travel/rue8)*. Next door, the *Art Salon Q3 (Hafenstr. 16 | art-salon-q3.com)* offers modern and colourful art.

BINZ/RÜGEN

Rügen – for most holidaymakers it simply means Binz. In Rügen's biggest and most fashionable seaside resort (pop. 5,100), one façade tries to outdo the other. Villas, Art Nouveau hotels and the spa house with its small towers: a dream in white.

There the beach is nearly secondary, until one sees it in its full glory and expanse – this is done best from the sea. Count along: one, two, three… and finally 370. That is the number of steps required until the viewing point at the end of the 🌀 Binz sea bridge. The promenade in the shadows of the trees lined slightly above it, is longer. It continues for 4.2 km/2.6 mi up to Prora; every few hundred metres exits lead to fine beach sand below, which extends far into the sea.

SIGHTSEEING

RESORT ARCHITECTURE ★

"Such beautiful squiggles everywhere", said the little girl, "Wilhelmine Art Nouveau", says the equally amazed architect. Both are correct: When you walk along the pedestrian zone towards the sea bridge or the beach promenade, one villa outshines the other, mostly white, some pale pink and timber-framed all over, nooks, small towers and bay windows. A special jewel, *Villa Undine (Strandpromenade 30)*, a dream made entirely from wood and is perhaps, apart from the spa house, the most fre-

RÜGENER, RANI, RÜGANER

They are called Merle, Lars or Mohammed: in the Baltic's Monday newspapers, parents proudly introduce their babies who have seen the light of day in the previous week. They may all call themselves Rüganer – those who move in later during early childhood, can never make it as far as Rügener. Real Rüganer claim that only people from Mönchgut, Wittow or Jasmund are actually on the island, apart from Hiddensee and Ummanz locals (and especially the residents from Stralsund!) There are also the Rani, originally a West Slavic tribe, who thrived in Rügen between the 7th and 14th centuries. Their god was Svantevit, had four heads and was worshipped in temples such as Jaromarsburg in Cape Arkona. During workdays the Rani robbed ships, as pirates they were similar to the Vikings. And real Rüganer.

Futuristic: not surprising that the rescue tower is being called the UFO

quently photographed. It was completed in 1908 and is also luxurious from the inside: you should at least eat a piece of cake here on the balcony in order to absorb the elegance of the golden twenties.

UFO

This building by Ulrich Müther at beach access 6, is officially the "Rescue Tower 2", but everyone only calls it the UFO. No wonder, it looks as if the concrete building on one leg (built in 1968) just floats above the dunes. Would you like to see it from the inside? No problem, for that you only have to get married: the Binz registry office uses the UFO as a branch office.

FISH SMOKEHOUSE

INSIDER TIP FISH-SMOKEHOUSE KUSE
In the fourth generation, the last fishermen in Binz smoke their catch, butterfish and mackerel, stremel-salmon and flounder. The Binz locals gladly stand in lines for it. *Daily 9am–8pm | At the fishing beach | Tel. 038393 29 70 | Budget*

SHOPPING

Where Margareten Street meets with the beach promenade, the *art mile starts (www.kunstmeile-binz.de)*. Galleries, a goldsmith and other artisans potter about peacefully here, side by side. Tastefully modest: the ceramic by *Tonicum (Margaretenstr. 20 | www.tonicum-keramik.de)*, often in marine tones. Just a few steps further is the glassblowing workshop, *Blumberg (daily 10am–6pm | Schillerstr. 11 | Tel. 03893 43 93 00 | www.blumberg-glas.de)*, where you don't only buy vases, glass animals and dazzling artworks, but can also under guidance **INSIDER TIP** blow a ball yourself. A perfect idea, and not only for kids either.

TRAVEL TIPS

Germany's Coasts: the most important information for your trip

ADMISSION

The admission fees provided in this guide apply to adults. Most establishments give discounts to children (often 50 percent), young people and families. At some establishments, e.g. animal parks, the entrance prices vary according to the seasons. Ask for group tariffs if needed!

BEACHES

To be in or near the water is a priority for most tourists at the Baltic Sea. There is the choice between natural beaches, sandy paradises, stretches of steep coast, or idyllic inland lakes. At the big beaches or official swimming areas, volunteer German Lifesaving Association lifeguards ensure the safety of swimmers and water sports enthusiasts, from June till mid-September.

BEACH CHAIRS

On colder days the beach chairs protect against wind or rain, on hot days from too much sun: you can't go wrong with renting a beach chair. Chairs are booked out fast during high season and should therefore be booked. The rental price depends on the season, and is around 7–12 euros/day or 35–65 euros/week. Information about suppliers is available at tourist info.

BERTHS

▶ BREMERHAVEN
In Bremerhaven cruise ships dock at a modern cruise ship terminal. From here Havenwelten can be reached on foot in about 30 minutes; shuttle buses are also available.

▶ HAMBURG
The Hamburg harbour has more than three cruise ship terminals: in HafenCity, in Altona and in Steinwerder since 2015.

▶ KIEL
The cruise ship docks are right in the centre which is a short distance away.

▶ LÜBECK/TRAVEMÜNDE
In Travemünde cruise ships dock at the East Prussia- and Scandinavia quay. The distance to the Lübeck city centre is about 15 km/9 mi.

▶ ROSTOCK-WARNEMÜNDE
Rostock-Warnemünde has a modern cruise ship terminal at the Warnemünde Cruise Centre. The centre of Warnemünde can be reached by foot and the Rostock city centre is approx. 15 km/9 mi away.

▶ SASSNITZ
In Sassnitz, cruise ships dock in Mukran harbour, about 7 km/4.5 mi from the centre.

Further docks are in Flensburg, Wismar and Binz.

FESTIVALS & EVENTS

MAY/JUNE

⭐ *Harbour birthday Hamburg (early May)*: excitement at the landing bridge with tall ships parade and tugboat ballet. hamburg.de/hafengeburtstag

INSIDERTIP *Elbjazz-Festival Hamburg:* the finest jazz at the harbour and in the Elbe Philharmonic Hall. www.elbjazz.de

Rum-Regatta: encounter historical sail ships at Flensburg's inner harbour (weekend after Ascension Day)

⭐ *Kiel week:* the biggest sailing sport event in the world with a huge supplementary program. The fjord bank becomes an action mile when you meet the 5,000 sailors there (last full June week).

JUNE–SEPT

Störtebeker-Festspiele in Ralswieck in Rügen the Störtebeker Festival takes place annually, where the history of the legendary pirates, Klaus Störtebeker and his men, the Victual Brothers, is enacted.

Barrel-beating: In Fischland-Darß-Zingst, the century-old tradition of barrel-beating is celebrated. Here riders try to beat pieces out of a hanging herring barrel with a club-like stick. www.fischland-darss-zingst.de

JULY/AUGUST

Hamburg Jazz Open: open-air jazz at Platen un Bomen. End of June | www.jazzbuero-hamburg.de

Hamburg "Jedermann" (everyman): open-air theatre in the Speicherstadt; for five weekends. Auf dem Sande | www.hamburger-jedermann.de

Travemünde Week: second biggest international sailing regatta with colourful social program (second half of July).

Flensburg Hofkultur (culture in the courtyards): festival with music, theatre and cabaret, film in the old craftsmen's and merchant's courtyards (mid-July–mid-Aug).

⭐ *Hanse Sail Rostock* always takes place during the second week in August is one of the biggest gatherings of traditional sailing ships in the Baltic Sea, with over 250 old ships. www.hansesail.com

SEPTEMBER

Reeperbahnfestival Hamburg: the neighourhood rocks in the music clubs. End of Sept. | www.reeperbahnfestival.com/en

Ironman 70.3 Rügen (eu.ironman.com) Only the toughest compete here in the mega triathlon.

SEPTEMBER/OCTOBER

Harbour Front Literature Festival Hamburg: The biggest reading festival in Northern Germany has fabulous event venues around the harbour, e.g. on the "MS Stubnitz" and the "Cap San Diego". www.harbourfront-hamburg.com

OCTOBER/NOVEMBER

Nordic Film Days: films from Northern Europe and Northern Germany in Lübeck's cinemas (end of Oct./beginning Nov five days)

POLAND

White beaches bordered by dunes and pine forest, rugged cliffs at which the storms gnaw away every autumn, lagoons, salt meadows and lagoons created by spits, half sea, half lagoon: Poland's Baltic coast has many faces.
It stretches 524 km/326 mi from the tip of Usedom island in the west, over the Gdansk bay up until the Vistula Spit, which peak is situated in Russian Kaliningrad.

North of Szczecin, the cliffs of the island of Wollin rise almost 100 m/328 ft – a massif out of chalk and clay, overgrown with beech and oak trees. Further to the east, the coastline drops and stretches into Western Pomerania's broad dune chains with never-ending beaches. Eventually it ascends again,

but now more smoothly, towards the Słowiński National Park, where the wind has piled up the sand to 50m high shifting sand dunes that can move up to 10m per year, depending on wind strength. This swimming paradise long ago stopped being a touristic desert anymore. The Baltic coast now ranks as one of the most popular holiday regions among the Polish. Small fishing villages from Rowy till Hel become crowded holiday destinations for sun-starved city dwellers, seaside resorts such as Międzyzdroje (Misdroy) on the Wollin island at the Szczecin lagoon with its beautiful beach and long beach promenade and Sopot in the Gdansk bay connect with the splendour and style of their fine past.

Gdansk and Gdynia – the two beautiful towns in the Baltic Sea have a lot to offer: harbour, seaside resort and Hanseatic architecture

GDANSK

Patrician houses that proclaim the spirit and prosperity of their creators, the harbour at the Motlawa River with the famous crane gate, winding cobblestone streets, the splendid Long Market, Dutch-influenced mannerism alongside Italian Renaissance – and above all, St. Mary's, the world's biggest brick church: Gdansk is a crown jewel of the Baltic cities.

The Old Town *(Główne Miasto)*, cultural centre and the part that was granted town status first, casts its spell over visitors year after year. You don't just admire a centrepiece of the Hanseatic power, but also a masterpiece of Polish restorers' art. The historical centre of Gdansk lay 90 percent in ruins and ashes in 1945. It was meticulously rebuilt, true to the original, according to old plans. The whole city centre is easy to explore on foot; therefore, no transport connections to these places are mentioned.

SIGHTSEEING

CRANE GATE (BRAMA ZURAW) ★
(🗺 8/C3)

In this gate, built in 1444 and flanked by two round towers, you can still see the huge treamills with which harbour workers and prisoners hosted loads up to 11 tons 11 m/ 36 ft high and raised the masts of large sailing ships. The Crane Gate was the biggest harbour crane in the world for a long time. Today it is the most photographed Gdansk landmark and the location of the *National Maritime Museum.*

LONG MARKET (DŁUGI TARG) ★
(🗺 8/C3)

The heart of the old town. Here, the most popular buildings of the historical Gdansk stand side by side, so artistically restored as if the city had never been destroyed, dominated by the *Town Hall* with its 80m high filigree tiered clock tower. The tip is crowned by a gilded statue of King Sigismund II Augustus. The Town Hall was built around 1330, in Gothic style, and has changed its appearance several times over the centuries. Gdansk's coat of arms is emblazoned above the portal. It has been restored to its original state by means of old plans. The *Museum of the Town History (Tue–Sun 10am–4pm | muzeumgdansk.pl)* is housed inside. Next to the Town Hall is the elevated *Artus Court (Dwór Artusa)*. The guild of the powerful Hanseatic merchants held their meetings and notorious banquets in the Mannerist-influenced palace, later the building housed the stock exchange. The showpiece of the big star-vaulted hall is a 12m high tiled stove: each of the 520 tiles is a hand-painted Delft original. In front of the Artus Court, water flows from one of the most photographed landmarks: finished in 1621, *Neptune Fountain (Fontanna Neptuana)* was created by the Flemish artists, Peter Husen and Johann Rogge. The gigantic sea god stretches the trident out. Not far from the fountain, the *Golden House (Złota Kamienica)* stands out from the row of houses north of the market, arguably the most beautiful merchant palace. It was built in 1609 for the

GDANSK GOLD WATER

One of the oldest European spirits originates from Gdansk. Its unusually beautiful trademark: 22 carat gold leaf flakes. They float like a snow blizzard in the clear, sweet spice-flavoured liqueur, and is still being produced today, based on its over 400-year-old secret recipe. Dutch chemist, Ambrosius Vermoellen, was the inventor of this brew with the precious ingredients. He founded a liqueur factory in Gdansk in 1598. Since the houses still displayed nature symbols instead of numbers, a sign of a salmon hung on Vermoellen's door. The factory and the increasingly famous Gold Water came to be known by the name used till today: the "salmon". Original Gdansk Gold Water contains – apart from the gold flakes – among others, juniper, coriander, cardamom, lavender, caraway and cinnamon. Up until today it is still found in many good restaurants in Gdansk, however, it is produced in Germany. A distillery in Nörten-Hardenberg has manufacturing rights.

Wonderfully restored houses show off at Long Market

former mayor, Jan Speymann. The rising Renaissance facade with stucco ornaments and bas-reliefs in green marble, is crowned by four antique figures – Antigone, Cleopatra, Oedipus and Achilles – like the Artus Court, it is the work of Flemish builder, Abraham van den Blocke.

LONG STREET (ULICA DŁUGA) ★
(㎶ 8/C3)

The boulevard between the Golden Gate and Long Market, lined with gorgeous gabled merchants' houses, is known as the "Royal Route", because rulers and kings entered the Old Town by Long Street. Today, vast numbers of tourists and locals stroll through the main street of the Old Town during the day; it is hard to imagine that everything here lay in ruins and ashes in 1945. The faithfully reconstructed *Lions Castle (Lwi Zamek | Długa 35)*, in which King Wladislaw lived when he was in town, as well as the famous *Uphagen's House* are well worth visiting. The baroque palace, built in 1776, of the Gdansk patrician and councillor, Johann Uphagen, is a museum today that recreates the life of a patrician family during the Rococo period, with a lot of original interior.

ST. MARY'S CHURCH (KOŚCIOŁ MARIACKI) ★ *(㎶ 8/C3)*

As if built for eternity, the biggest brick building of the world towers over the Old Town behind the Town Hall. 25 000 people can be accommodated in the 105m long and 68m wide three-nave church. The filigree nets and star vaults, the white painted interior and the magically enhanced incoming light through 37 enormous windows give an overwhelming spatial impression. Most of the interior decoration from earlier times got lost in the war. The Gothic *main altar* and the Gdansk *Beautiful Madonna* from the 15th century, in the St. Anne's chapel, are among the preserved treasures.

One of the most precious treasures of the St. Mary's church is the *astronomical clock*. The 12m high instrument from 1470 has a complicated calendar and a sky disc. In order to prevent the master, Hans Düringer, from making a similar clock for another town, Gdansk locals gouged his eyes out. The organ of the Lord's house tells of an eventful history. The instrument was made in 1985 by the organ building company Hillebrand (Altwarnbüchen) and is based on the model of the baroque Frisian organ. A Gdansk native doctor, Otto Kulcke, founded a supporting association for its restoration. Organ concerts in St. Mary's church are a magnificent sound experience. Dare to climb up the ✴ tower. There are more than 400 steps, but from the 78m gallery, the town is at your feet in all its beauty. *Mon–Sun 9am–5pm, Sun 1pm–5pm | www.bazylikamariacka.pl*

ST. MARY'S STREET (ULICA MARIACKA) ★ *(📖 8/C3)*

In St. Mary's Street, which leads from the women's gate to the St. Mary's church, a hint of old Gdansk hovers. The merchants' houses are lined by raised terraced-like front buildings – the famous Beischlägen. Extended storage cellars originated from the 16th century as street entrances and slowly became status symbols of the rich patricians. The front buildings flourished into magnificent decorated porches where business was discussed; in the summer they dined with family and also watched the hustle and bustle on the street. Their cellars house handicraft shops, galler-

The tower of the St. Mary's church rises powerfully over the rows of houses

SHOPPING

Apart from shopping malls there are also many small retailers

Sundays after church you'll actually find Gdansk locals busy shopping. Since there is no law governing trading hours, the big malls are actually busy on Sundays.

One of the biggest and newest Gdansk shopping centres is the *Galeria Bałtyca.* Both Polish branded clothing as well as international designer collections are offered. Other malls are also at the outskirts of town, and are open Mondays till Saturdays 9am – 9pm, Sundays 10am – 8pm. Food such as fruit, vegetables, mushrooms, meat and fish can be purchased in the historical Gdansk market hall *(Hala Targowa)*: inside and on the beaches in front of the hall fresh products and flowers are on offer Mondays to Fridays from early morning till 6pm *(Saturdays till at least 3pm)*. Most of the businesses in Sopot have settled in the Monte Cassino Street and in the casino at the *Przyjaciół Sopotu* square: souvenirs, antiques, expensive boutiques and small food shops. The most popular shopping street in *Gdynia* is the *Ulica Świętojańska*. In the new shopping centre, *Klif (Aleia Zwycięstwa 256 | www.gdynia.klif.pl/en)*, at the *Gdynia Orłowo* train station, there are all kinds of clothing in the most fashionable brands alongside the shops.

LOW BUDGET

CCC (Ulica Szuberta 102 a | Morena shopping centre | galeriamorena.pl | ZKM-Bus 142: Galeria Morena): You can't buy your new shoes for cheaper than here anywhere else in the town. The Polish brands offer many designs.

Fashion House Outlet Center (Ulica Przywidzka 8 | www.designeroutlets.pl | ZKM-Bus 174, 574: Fashion House): Popular branded clothes are by up to 70 percent, among others, Nike, Puma, Adidas and Rossignol. Italian shoes and Polish brands from older collections at very attractive prices.

TRAVEL WITH KIDS

AQUAPARK SOPOT
Open and covered swimming pools, a wild river, gigantic slides and cascades are what the Sopot Aquapark offers. While you enjoy the sun on the terrace, or one of the new saunas on the first floor of the recreation centre, your child can swim and play under the watchful eyes of a lifeguard. The Aqua restaurant is on site. Find Info and opening hours on www.aquaparksopot.pl

ies and the most beautiful but also the most expensive amber workshops in the city.

FOOD & DRINK

KUBICKI
For almost a hundred years, the traditional restaurant has been at the old fish market. Newly renovated, it is rustic-elegant with fine Polish cuisine and also many Kashubian specialities. Beautiful outside spaces with a view of the ↘ Motlawa River. ul. Wartka 5 | Tel 5 83 01 00 50 | www.restauracjakubicki.pl | Moderate

CAFÉ PELLOWSKI
A true paradise for sweet teeth: in the café of Gdansk's most traditional pastry shop, you can indulge in a huge selection of delicious cakes and tarts. ul. Długa 40/42 | Tel. 5 83 01 45 20 | Budget

INSIDER TIP PROLOGUE
Opened in 2015 and instantly ended up at the top of the Gdansk restaurant scene. Excellent food: fusion cooking in the form of imaginative creations (goats' cheese in puff pastry). Harmonious brick ambience. ul. Grodzka 9 (close to the fish market) | Tel. 5 85 26 59 09 | www.prologue.pl | Moderate

WHERE TO GO

OLIWA (OLIVA) ★
The once independent town at the hill top of the Trojmiasto forest park, 15 km /9.3 mi west of Gdansk, hides a church music treasure: Oliwa cathedral – the early Gothic cathedral of a Cistercian monastery founded in the 12th century, houses a famous Rococo organ from 1763. It took 20 years to make the instrument, and it has been modified and enhanced many times over the following decades. Today its 7,880 pipes and 100 stops produce a wonderful sound. While the organ pipes sound, carved angel figures with trombones and bells move. In the summer there are hourly INSIDER TIP short performances, daily from 10am to 4pm. Just behind the cathedral is a big picturesque park from the 18th century, where impressive classical concerts are performed. The Rococo influenced Bishop's Palace is also worth seeing (Pałac Opatóv). Next door in the old granary of the monastery is the Kashubian Ethnographic Park (Muzeum Etnograficzne) | Tue–Sun 10am–4pm.

GDYNIA

Before the first World War, Gdynia was a small fishing village. The unrivalled fast growth began when the place became the most important harbour of the newly founded Republic of Poland after the first World War: within a few decades the population increased to 240 000. The huge harbour area characterises the youngest town of the Polish Baltic coast. It does not offer brick Gothic and Baroque attractions, of course, but the Bauhaus style influences modern *city* with businesses, atmospheric cafés and restaurants along both boulevards, *Starowiejska* and *Świętojańska*.

The floating restaurant, *Viking II (al. Zjednoczenia | Tel. 5 86 61 46 21 | Moderate)*, in a reconstructed Viking boat, is original, situated at the southern pier next to the museum ships. For pub crawling nothing really tops *Donegal pub (ul. Zgoda 10 | Tel.5 86 20 46 23 | Budget)*, a quaint bit of Ireland in the middle of Gdynia, mostly a crowdy and great atmosphere. The *Witold Gombrowicz City Theatre (www. teatrgombrowicza.art.pl)* moves to the INSIDER TIP summer stage at Orłowo beach every year. The atmospheric performances from Shakespeare to classic concerts on the open-air stage, are unique to the Polish Baltic Sea. The new *Sea Tower (Hryniewickiego 6 | Tel. 5 86 25 95 56 | www.seatowersgdynia. pl | Expensive)* is spectacular, on 142m it is the highest building on the Polish coast.

A trip to Gdynia is worth it, but most of all because of the impressive *Oceanographic Museum (May–Aug Tue–Sun 9am–7pm, otherwise 10am–5pm | al. Zjednoczenia 1 | www.akwarium.gdynia. pl)*: sea turtles, colourful tropical fish, piranhas and sharks frolic in 30 big sea water aquariums. *Information: pl Konstytucji 1, central station | Tel. 5 86 28 54 66 | www.gdynia.pl*

In front of Gdynia's down-to-earth and modern scenery, historical ships also anchor

FOOD & DRINK

Gdansk offers a combination of old Polish cuisine and European dishes

When you feel like traditional Polish cuisine, then Gdansk will definitely not disappoint.

Whether at an expensive exclusive restaurant or low budget bar, pierogi (the traditionally filled *dumplings*), borscht (red beetroot soup) or zurek (sour soup), are almost always on the menu. The *Kashubian Cuisine* has also significantly influenced the Gdansk restaurants. Most of all, herrings are served in all kinds of varieties – in sour cream, in oil, or with garlic, cucumbers and onions. And of course, the Baltic Sea food is also part of Gdansk cuisine: *fish dishes* can be found almost everywhere.

After Poland had joined the EU, the Polish cuisine was definitely Europeanised and internationalised: it has become more versatile, and more and more restaurants have opened that serve fusion-cuisine. *Sushy bars* are currently trendy, but vegetarian options are still quite scarce.

The service has gained quality in recent years. The ubiquitous socialistic attitude of a few years ago has been replaced by the motto "the customer is king", came about, and the patron experiences it. During weekends and afternoons, affordable lunch menus are served.

LOCAL SPECIALITIES

Babka – yeast cakes with raisins and glazed fruit, served with icing or chocolate glaze

Borscht – red beet soup

Chłodnik – cold red beet soup with sour milk

Gold Water – sweet herb liqueur with anise flavour and gold flakes

Kotlety schabowe – thin, crumbed pork schnitzel

Makowiec – poppy seed cake

Naleśniki – pancakes with quark, marmalade or meat filling

Pierogi – dumplings, mostly with meat or cabbage filling

Rosół – chicken, turkey or beef broth with vegetables, traditionally served with noodles

Sernik – cheese cake, sometimes with raisins or glazed fruit

TRAVEL TIPS

Poland: the most important information for your trip

BERTHS

▶ **GDANSK**

The Gdansk harbour is certainly the biggest in Poland, however, only small ships can dock here.

▶ **GDYNIA**

Big cruise ships anchor here, also when the excursion destination is Gdansk, which is 30 km/19 mi away.

ENTRY

For EU citizens and Swiss citizens, the identity card will suffice, children need their own I.D. with nationality endorsement and photograph.

HEALTH

Don't forget to bring your European Health Insurance Card. It is accepted at the public health care services. Should you first have to pay doctors' and chemist fees in cash, submit the receipt at your local point of sale once you have returned. In event of an emergency, go to a hospital emergency room *(pogotowie)*.

MONEY

Automatic tellers are practically around every corner. Most shops and restaurants accept all major credit cards.
The Polish currency is the zloty (1 zloty = 100 groszy), it is freely convertible, that is, the exchange rate changes. Everyday necessities are mostly cheaper than in the UK and the US, cigarettes and vodka are much cheaper, imported goods cost the same and are sometimes also more expensive.

TELEPHONE & MOBILE

Telephone booths function with telephone cards *(carta telefoniczna)*. These can be obtained (in denominations of 25 – 100 units) at kiosks, petrol stations and post office branches. Mobile phones can be used without problems in Poland. Since June 2017, the roaming charges have been cancelled throughout the EU, which means that someone who uses a British mobile phone supplier in Poland and wants to contact a mobile phone with a British sim card, should dial the number without the country code.

BUDGETING

Coffee	from £1.4/$1.7
	for one espresso at a café
Light meal	from £4.5/$5.5
	for a toasted cheese and tomato
Admission	£1.5-5/$2-6
	at most museums

LITHUANIA

The Estonians and Latvians are completely different, more emotional and more southern: the Lithuanians are a bit like the Italians of the Baltic region. This is perhaps a bit exaggerated. Though it is the biggest of the three Baltic Sea Republics, about the same size as Bavaria, with 3.4 million residents, it differs from its neighbours in some respects.

Lithuanians are catholic. This is due to its shared history with Poland. Here, lived religion is a natural component of everyday culture, with the impressive double towers that characterise the towns and villages throughout the whole country. In many places crucifixes and statues of Mary line the streets and alleys. Strong nature worship is also typical of the Lithuanians. The forest is

Lithuania's big myth. Curiously, this love for nature is rooted in the old pagan-pantheistic beliefs. For a long time, the Baltic Sea nation resisted the crusades of the Teutonic knights and remained unbaptised up until the 14th century. The Lithuanians talk about it fondly and proudly that they were the last pagans in Europe. Nowhere else in the Baltic region is the summer solstice so extensively celebrated.

Lithuania offers a large variety of landscapes: the Aukštaitija lake district in the north-east, mineral springs in the south, the small country has more than 750 rivers, and a third of it is forested. The coast only measures 99 km/62 mi, but features one of the most famous Baltic Sea landscapes: the Curonian Spit.

Photo: the Curonian Spit is a unique piece of Baltic Sea nature

Sea sand: Holidaymakers have been relaxing at the beaches of the biggest Baltic country for centuries

The Republic of Lithuania has a multi-ethnic history. This country has always connected east and west. It was certainly one of the reasons why the stunningly beautiful Baroque town, Vilnius, the capital city, was awarded the title "European capital of culture" in 2009.

KLAIPĖDA

Klaipėda (pop. 195,000), located at the mouth of the Curonian Lagoon in the Baltic Sea, is Lithuania's "gateway to the world". The economical engine and pivotal to the upswing in the country's third largest city has now experienced for years is the port.

In Klaipėda, German and Lithuanian history merge. For almost seven centuries, from its establishment in 1252 till the end of the war in 1945, the town was called Memel and was part of East Prussia. In the small Old Town, with its chessboard-pattern streets, the warehouses and half-timbered houses, the charm

FOOD & DRINK

Where Sauerkraut meets orange-ginger: traditional Baltic and the young culinary scene

Steamy *potato dumplings* filled with minced meat or bacon, and covered in a *bacon and cream sauce*? Traditional Baltic cuisine is not really recommended for a diet, it is *hearty*, rural and quite calorie-dense. However, you have other options between Tallinn, Rīga and Klaipėda. How about a grilled salmon steak with a wasabi coating? Or perhaps rather a portion of *pancakes* with a light dill cream cheese filling?

The three Baltic Sea republics reached a *culinary turning point* long ago. The orientation towards the west certainly came by, as the saying has it, "looking farther than your own plate". Since then, a young, fresh, constantly changing restaurant scene has flourished, especially in the major cities. And creative as the Balts simply are, young star chefs like Imre Kose in his Tallinn restaurant, Vertigo, or Mārtiņš Rītiņš happily combine the exotic with country-specific native dishes and ingredients. *Fusion cuisine* is trendy. Imre Kose improves sauerkraut, an Estonian classic, with orange and ginger: a traditional modern interpretation.

In addition, *international* cuisine has been accepted. Whether Mexican spiciness or fine nouvelle cuisine, *Asiatic* or *Mediterranean*: if you like, you can try a different direction in the Baltic metropolis every day of your holiday. The Estonians, Latvians and Lithuanians, especially the younger generation, have changed their eating habits. *Good food* has become important and part of a new *cultural experience*.

LOCAL SPECIALITIES

Blynai, Blyneliai (Lithuania) – pancakes with meat, quark or mushroom filling

Kringel (Estonia/Latvia) – sweet pretzel-formed almond pastry

Cepelinai (Lithuania) – star among Baltic dishes: filled with quark or meat, airship formed boiled potato dumplings; covered with bacon, cream and onions (also *Didžkukuliai*)

NO LITHENGLISH, PLEASE!

Lithuania has instituted a ten-member language inspection that persecutes lawbreakers with too loose language. The local language law for example stipulates that Lithuanian should not only be used without error, but also without anglicisms and other foreign words. For instance, e-mail is called Elektroninis paštas. The inspectors impose fines up until 1,500 litas against editors and moderators who make too many mistakes. After all, Lithuanian is an old and small language that needs to be especially cherished. However, in everyday life everyone in Lithuania can say what comes to mind, and the inspectors are powerless against anglicisms such as *Biznismenis* (businessmen) or *Surprizas* (surprise).

of the old Hanseatic town of Memel is still tangible. After the war, the city got its early medieval Lithuanian settlement name back, as it first emerged from a dark history in the 9th century: Klaipėda.

SIGHTSEEING

LINDEN STREET (LIEPŲ GATVĖ)
(*9/D2*)

Behind the Exchange Bridge on the northern shore of the Danė, the most beautiful street in the New Town (laid out in 1770) branches off, it has preserved a lot of its pre-war charm. The neo-Gothic *central post office* (1893) is a landmark, the carillon in the bell tower sounds weekend afternoons with the popular melody from "Annie from Tharau". Next door in the *clock museum (Laikrodžiu muziejus | Tue–Sun noon–6pm | Liepų 12r)*, timekeepers from the hour glass to the atomic chronometer can be seen.

INSIDER TIP MERIDIANAS (*9/C3*)

On the Danė shore, a floating landmark of Klaipėda, the three-masted Meridianas is now moored again after a long stay in the shipyard. Built in 1947 in Turku, Finland, the wooden barquentine served as a sailing school ship on the Baltic Sea for the Klaipeda maritime academy. It was decommissioned after an accident, and became a canteen after a while and also really scruffy. When it was towed into the shipyard it was saved at the last minute. At the end of 2014, the proud tall ship reopened, this time as a noble restaurant with recommendable ship's bar. A part of the Meridianas is a museum *(tours/reservations Tel. 61 80 06 39 | www.pasazas.lt/en)*, one can visit the museum.

The theatre in the Old Town of Klaipėda

OLD TOWN (SINAMIESTIS)
(⏢ 9/A–B, 3–4)

Between the small shops, cafés and galleries, everyday life drifts past very tranquilly. The Old Town grew as a trade district.

This is evident from the street names: there is a Fisherman (Žvejų), a Shoemaker (Kurpių) and a Baker (Kepėjų) Street, and Locksmiths (Šaltkalvių) and Blacksmiths (Kalvių) each have their own street as well. In the *Didžioji Vandens* (large waterway), the *Lithuania Minor museum (Mažosios Lietuvos Istorios Muziejus |Tue–Sat 10am–6pm | D. vandens 6 | www.mlimuziejus.lt/en)* covers a wide area of the East-Prussian and Lithuanian cultural history. The small but original Blacksmith museum *(Kalvystės muzejus |Tue–Sat 10am–6pm | Šaltkalvių 2)* is worth a visit.

THREATRE SQUARE (TEATRO AIKŠTĖ)
(⏢ 9/A3)

It is the central square of the Old Town. The *Simon Dach Fountain*, with an Annie from Tharau *(Taravos Anikė)* sculpture is at the centre. It is the figure of a woman, representing the woman about whom the poet from Memel, Simon Dach, wrote the poem with the same name.

SHOPPING

Klaipėda's main shopping streets are the *H. Manto* and the *Tiltu*. Interesting shops are in, for example, the Friedrich-Passage *(Tiltų26 a)*. Handicrafts and amber can mostly be bought in the Old Town and from street hawkers at the Theatre Square. The bookshop, *Akademija (Daukanto 16)* has city maps and good country maps.

AUTENTIC

Large selection of amber jewellery and Spit souvenirs, directly at the Exchange Bridge. *Zveju 4*

INSIDER TIP GALERIJA PĖDA

In this gallery you can obtain stylish jewellery made by Lithuanian artist

Klaipėda almost appears dreamy in the soft light

Vytautas Karćiauskas; it comes at a price. During weekends piano music accompanies shopping and viewing.
Daily 10am – 7pm | Turgaus 10 | www.karciauskas.com

CENTRAL MARKET (TURGAUS)
From 6am – 6pm daily, fish, meat, dairy products, fruit and vegetables, honey and everything from the garden and the woods is offered for sale.
Turgaus aikšte

WHERE TO GO

CURONIAN SPIT (KURŠIŲ NERIJA) ⭐
Shifting sand dunes up to 70m high, picturesque fishing villages, pine forests and a never-ending beach: the Curonian Spit is undoubtedly one of the most bizarre and most beautiful coastal landscapes in Europe. Almost 100 km/62 mi long and only 350m wide at its narrowest part, the Spit separates the Baltic Sea from the Curonian Lagoon, a freshwater lagoon that is three times as big as Lake Constance. Today the Curonian Spit's land is divided. The north belongs to Lithuania, the southern half to the Russian enclave Kaliningrad (Königsberg). Both sides have declared the Spit as a national park, in 2001 UNESCO added it as a World Heritage Site. Respect the strict protective directives! Ferries leave from Klaipėda to the Spit.
Schedule: www.keltas.lt/en

INSIDER TIP ▸ HILL OF WITCHES (RAGANOS KALNAS)
The hill of witches is situated at Juodkrante, halfway between Nida and Klaipėda. Along a circular trail (45 minutes), around a forested hill, Lithuanian artists have lovingly set up carved wooden spirits, witches and goblins.

BERTH

▸ **KLAIPĖDA**
In Klaipėda cruise ships dock at the cruise ship terminal. The centre is 1 km/0.6 mi away.

Begin at the thoroughfare, which is the L. Rézos gatvė, at nr. 48 at the roadside the wooden witch with the axe shows the way.

PALANGA
The Lithuanian spa- and seaside resort (pop. 20,000) was well known throughout the whole Soviet Union in those days. Today many Russians and Latvians still travel to the former Polangen, recently more and more Germans. But most of all, the Lithuanians have their holidays here during the short Lithuanian swimming season. In July and August, the hotels, discos and bars are very busy. Palanga's life axis is the *Basanavičiaus* gatvė, the sea end of the pier protrudes 600m into the sea.

ŽEMAITIJA NATIONAL PARK
A 220 km²/85 mi² slice of picturesque Baltic comprising forest and glacial ridges, 65 rivers, 7 crystal clear lakes. It is Lithuania's youngest national park (60 km/37 mi east of Palanga), a paradise for nature enthusiasts, canoeists and hikers. *Plateliai* is at the centre of the park, there you will also find the tourist information *(Didzioji 8 | Tel. 448 4 92 31 | www.zemaitijosnp.lt/en)* At *Plokštinė*, a former nuclear missile silo has been turned into a *museum (May–Sept Tue–Sun 9am–5pm)*. Until 1987, Soviet intercontinental missiles were kept in the 30m deep shafts.

LATVIA

Almost 500 km/311 mi of coastline, untouched natural landscape of eastern melancholic vastness, mansions and weathered castle ruins that bear witness to lost foreign rule and an eventful history: Latvia (pop. 2.4 million), in the middle of the three Baltic Sea Republics, is perhaps characterised most strongly by these contrasts and this atmosphere, which is typical of the Baltic region.

In some places it seems like time is standing still — especially in the countryside. Time passes by faster in the Latvian capital: Rīga has been transformed into a pulsating Baltic Sea metropolis, elegant and extravagant, combining stunning brick Gothic with the splendour of Art Nouveau, which in Europe's most lavish industrial expansion districts has developed into a stone operetta. The beautiful "Miss Baltica" casts her spell over every visitor.

RĪGA

With nearly 1 million residents, Rīga likes to claim being the only real big city in the Baltic region. For Latvia it is the capital city, heart and soul. Every third resident of the country lives here.

This pulsating metropolis on the Daugava River will also enthrall travellers. *Vecrīga*, the dandified Old Town with its winding alleys, churches, old monastery, merchants' and guild houses and the famous Art Nouveau district of the New Town combines an 800-year history of

A metropolis and rural province: the country in the middle of the Baltic region is still in search of its own identity

so many architectural masterpieces that Unesco elevated it to World Heritage Status as the "Paris of the east" in 1997. But Rīga is also a changing city. Wherever you look in the city, buildings are being built, renovated and restored. Even though there was an economic crisis in 2009 and the banks and investments in property took a hard blow, it only lasted a short while after the real end of the boom. Property prices that shot up irrationally high in the previous years, dropped considerably. Rīga is still an ex-pensive place. Most of Riga's inhabitants therefore live in neighbourhoods which tourists are unlikely to wander into: the grey suburbs disfigured by Soviet apartment blocks. As soon as the sun is a bit a higher in the Spring, "Miss Baltica" springs to life again. Everywhere between the cathedral-, Līvu- and the Town Hall square, shops and street cafés invite you to enjoy the day in this wonderful town. Rīga's historical Old Town is closed for motor vehicles, but all attractions can be comfortably explored on foot.

SIGHTSEEING

Rīga has more than 50 museums, which does not include exhibitions in the many galleries. A current overview is available from the tourism information and on *www.muzeji.lv*

ART NOUVEAU DISTRICT ★
(🗺 *10/B–C1*)

In Rīga's New Town at the beginning of the 20th century, during the economic boom, most of the nearly 800 Art Nouveau houses for which the town is so famous, were built on both sides of the wide Brīvības boulevard. Latvian and Russian architects led by Mikhail Eisenstein created the euphoria of the *national Romanticism* in entire streets, in operetta splendour. The most beautiful Belle Epoque buildings are in the following streets: *Alberta* (2–13), *Elizabetes* (10

b, 33), *Audēju* (7–11) and *Strēlnieku* (4 a). The Old Town also has magnificent Art Nouveau houses in *Skārņu* (1–3, 6–10) and *Šķūņu* Street (10, 12). The INSIDER TIP *Rīga Art Nouveau Centre (Tue – Sun 10am – 6pm | Alberta 12 | www.jundendstils.riga.lv)* offers Art Nouveau exhibitions and events.

CASTLE (RĪGAS PILS) (🗺 *10/B2*)

Constructed in 1330, it has been destroyed many times and was finally rebuilt in 1515. The *Holy Spirit Tower* and the northern castle wall are the oldest sections of the castle. In the 18th and 19th centuries it was rebuilt on a larger scale. Today, the castle is the seat of the president and houses the Latvian *National History Museum (Mon–Sun 11am–7pm | www.history-museum.lv)*. Furthermore, the *Museum of Foreign Art and the Museum of Literature, Theatre and Music is also here. Pils laukums 3*

One – no, three – of Riga's landmarks: the Three Brothers

SHOPPING

Balm for body and soul: a variety of souvenirs rooted in vibrant craftsmanship

The Baltic region has long since arrived in Europe in terms of its (super) market economy. From Narva to Marijampole, discounters dominate the shopping world and offer a range of goods that is in no way inferior to the west.

On the contrary, shopping centres such as the gigantic Akropolis in Vilnius or the Viru keskes at the Tallin gates are otherwise only found in America. In these shopping temples as big as aircraft hangars, with up to 80 cash registers, wrapped in steel-glass architecture and surrounded by shopping streets with boutiques, Baltic families spend whole days. Most shopping centres are open till late at night, many even till midnight and seven days a week.

SOUVENIRS

Whoever looks for a Baltic souvenir will find something in each of the three countries. In Lithuania there is of course hardly any way past the "gold of the Baltic Sea." The amber masters in this country are real experts of their trade. Amber is for sale in almost every souvenir shop in Lithuania, the biggest and most beautiful choice can be found at the coast, at the *Guild of Palanga Amber* jewellers, mostly in Nida at the Curonian Spit. The Lithuanians have always been famous for wood carvings, it is the oldest tradition of their folk art inspired by nature. In Latvia and Estonia, traditional handicraft is widespread, from woven, finely embroidered to somewhat scratchy linen tablecloths, but the original knitted pullovers by the *Khino* trois from the ethnic island, Kihnu, are among the most beautiful.

During times when tourism flourishes, many artisans specialise in souvenirs. The most beautiful range from all three countries can be found in the large ethnographic open-air museum. Or visit one of the handicraft markets which are open during the same time as many of Baltic Folk fests.

FREEDOM MONUMENT (BRĪVĪBAS PIEMINEKLIS) ★ (⑂ 10/C2)

National Landmark. The gracious girl figure, "Milda", lifts three golden stars towards the sky from her 42m high column. They symbolise the Latgale, Kurzeme and Vidzeme provinces – Latvia's national unity. The monument, erected in 1935, with the inscription *Tevzemei un Brīvībai* ("For Fatherland and Freedom"), was a thorn in the eye to the Soviets, and they could not wait to lay their hands on it. *Brīvības bulvāris*

ST. MARY'S CATHEDRAL (DOMA BAZNĪCA) ★ (⑂ 10/B2)

The biggest church of the Baltic region emerged as a result of work commissioned by the city founder, Bischof Albert (his statue is in the cathedral courtyard). In view of its planned dimensions, Albert laid the cornerstone outsides the city walls in 1211. The shell alone, with its 2m thick walls, took 50 years, and thereafter the cathedral was renovated so many times that its architecture combines three eras: Romanesque, Gothic and finally Baroque, from which the splendid features of the pulpit and the pews from the Brotherhood of Blackheads stem. The *Walcker organ* from 1884 is a grand masterpiece, with 6718 pipes, and – after the completed restoration – one of the biggest and best-sounding organs in the world again. *Tue–Fri 1pm – 6pm, Sat 10am – 2pm | Organ concerts Wed and Fri 7pm | Concert ticket office opposite the west portal | Tel. 67 21 32 13 | www.doms.lv*

THREE BROTHERS (TRĪS BRĀLI) (⑂ 10/B2)

These three are actually not siblings. Even though they are so close together, they were built at completely different times. House no. 17 with the Gothic stepped gables to the far right, is from the 15th century and is so to say, the "big brother", it is regarded as the oldest residential building in Rīga. In contrast, the yellow gable in the middle bears Dutch Baroque characteristics and dates back to 1646. The brother no. 19 on the left is from the 18th century, and houses the Latvian *Museum of Architecture (Mon – Fri 9am – 5pm | www.archmuseum.lv). Mazā Pils 17 – 21*

JEWISH MUSEUM (ZIDU MUZ EJS) (⑂ 10/C1)

Before the Second World War, the Jewish community in Rīga (5 percent) was the second biggest minority in Latvia, after the Russians (10 percent). But of the total 44,000 Jewish citizens, only 175 survived the the Holocaust. The historian Margers Westermanis, a survivor himself, has impressively documented the lives of the Jews in Latvia. *So–Do 12–17 Uhr | Eintritt frei | Skolas 6 | www.jews.lv*

INSIDER TIP ▶ KALNCIEMA QUARTER

At the western shore of the Daugava is a part of Rīga which no tourist is likely to wander into: panel blocks and tenements characterise the appearance of Pārdaugava. There are also almost 2,000 wooden houses, many more than in other European towns. A unique project of the Baltic region is growing here: the *Kalnciema Quarter (www.kalnciemaiela.lv). Since the brothers Kārlis and Mārtinš Dambergs began to restore some semi-dilapidated wooden houses on Kalnciema Street, with the mix of fantasy, courage and pioneering spirit typical of Latvian young entrepreneurs, this has become Riga's liveliest, trendiest neighbourhood. *Restaurant Maia*, which opened there, already enjoys cult status; in the café next door, Latvia's top chef,

Figures and ornaments adorn the facades of the Art Nouveau district

Mārtiņš Rītiņš, dishes up his slow food compositions. There is a *gallery* where exhibitions are alternated every two weeks, an exclusive wine shop, chic offices transformed from ruined buildings and inhabited by architects and designers. On Saturdays there is a *farm produce* and *arts* and *craft market (10am – 4pm)*, there are concerts every Thursday, mostly "for free and outside". Events are advertised on Facebook and Twitter, where the small cultural district already has 30,000 followers: Kalnciema Quarter in Rīga is now ultra hip. It is worth it to explore the streets around the Pārdaugava district, with its weathered villas from the boom times, wild parks and old wooden houses, partly severely derelict and partly restored. This is a Rīga so completely different from the postcard beauty of Art Nouveau and Old Town. Tramline 10 goes to Pārdaugava from the Old Town *(central station, Schützen Square)*.

INSIDER TIP **MOSCOW SUBURB (MASKAVAS FORŠTATE)** *(⬚ 10/B3)*

Behind the main train station, on both sides of the Gogola iela (street), the town image changes: old Russian houses line the streets, everything appears a bit nostalgic. Since time immemorial, Russians and many Jewish merchants as well as Rīga inhabitants have been living here. The district is dominated by the *Latvian Academy of Sciences*, a high-rise building in the monumental style of the Stalin era. An interesting building stands in Elijas Street: the classic *Jesus Church (Jezus lut. Baznīca)*, the biggest wooden building in the Baltic region. A bit further, at the *Gogola/Dzirnavu Street* intersection, a memorial commemorates the nearly 30,000 Rīga Jews who were rounded up in a ghetto by the Nazis in the fall of 1941 and were subsequently shot in the woods outside the city.

Meanwhile, Old Russian religiousness lives under the golden dome of the *Grebenschtschikow Church (Grebenščikova baznīca)* in the *M. Krasta Street* in the eastern part of the suburb. *Daily services 8am and 5 pm*

MUSEUM OF THE HISTORY OF RĪGA AND NAVIGATION (RĪGAS VĒSTURES UN KUG'NIECĪBAS MUZEJS)
(🗺 10/B3)

One of the oldest museums in the whole of Europe and the biggest in Latvia at the same time. This museum includes a rich collection of city history and art. Part of the building was previously the cathedral school where Johann Gottfried Herder once taught and founded his famous folk song collections, in which he also recorded some Latvian Dainas. His bust is on the Herderplatz in front of the museum. *May–Sept daily 11am–5pm, otherwise Wed–Sun 11am–5pm | Tours also in English, book at 67 35 66 76 | Palasta 4 | www.rigamuz.lv*

ST. PETER'S CHURCH (PĒTERBAZNĪCA)
(🗺 10/B3)

Rīga's highest and most beautiful church was first built as a wooden building back in 1209. The 123,5m high metal ✄ tower was completed in 1973 and characterises the town view. *Tue–Sun 10am–5pm | Skārņu 19 | www.peterbaznica.lv*

CAFÉS

INSIDER TIP MIIT-CAFE

Here one can order an espresso and then hire a city bike: the hip shop serves as a café as well as a bicycle rental service. Vegetarian menu, good coffee! *Lačpleša 10 | Tel. 26 77 54 90 | www.miit.lv | Budget*

INSIDER TIP OSIRIS

Popular café for breakfast, lunch and dinner – or for just a drink in between. Comfortable atmosphere with classical music. Popular artists' meeting place. *Barona 31 | Tel. 67 24 30 02 | Moderate–Expensive*

Rīga's castle

SHOPPING

Rīga's city is one shopping mile. In the Old Town there are several boutiques, in the other, superfine shops have settled in the Torna. Noble labels of the fashion scene can be found at the elegant Elizabetes. Tērbates, in the new city, along with its side streets, is turning into a trendy shopping district for designer fashion, jewellery and cosmetics.

WHERE TO GO

JŪRMALA ★

20 km/12 mi from Rīga's gates are the Baltic Sea – and the seaside resort, Jūrmala (pop. 60, 000). A small town

The Turaida castle is located amidst green landscape

that was discovered by Rīga residents as an elegant spa and seaside resort at the turn of the 19th and the 20th centuries. The cheerful wooden houses in the Dzintari, Dubulti and Majori districts are relics of those times and are being sold at maximum prices today. The fine, white beach that stretches along the coast for more than 30 km/19 mi, the shallow water and the long promenade lure the people.

SIGULDA ★

The small town (35 km/22 mi southwest of Cēsis) is the tourist centre of the national park. The Gauja River cuts especially deep into the sandstone rocks and at its shores, it washes into Latvia's most beautiful and biggest caves: the big Devil's Cave (Lielā Velnala), the Victor's Cave (Viktorala) and the 20m deep Gutman's Cave, shrouded in myth (Gūtmaņa ala). Sigulda is popular countrywide for its castles that line the val-

ley ravine like crenellations: *Turaida* and *Krimulda*. The bishop's castle, Turaida, overlooked the Gauja since 1213, until it was destroyed in the Great Northern War. Detailed reconstruction began in 1953. From the 30m high ☀ castle keep, there is a fantastic view of a part of this 917 km²/354 mi² biggest national park of the Baltic region. The view from the ☀ INSIDER TIP ▶ cable car, which runs from Sigulda to Krimulda castle is even more breathtaking. In the town itself, the new castle and the old Ordensburg are worth seeing.

BERTH

▶ **RĪGA**
Cruise ships dock at the Rīga passenger terminal, which is 1 km/0.6 mi from the Old Town.

ESTONIA

Estonia (EST: Eesti) is something like the Scandinavia of the Baltic region. In nature everything seems more Nordic, coniferous forests characterise the landscape and the enormous moors inhabited by moose. People – geographically, linguistically and mentally – feel very connected to neighbouring Finland. Estonians are considered individualists. They are quiet people, taciturn and introverted. Here they refer to the Baltic Sea as the "Western Sea."

Estonia is the smallest of the three republics, but its winding, island-rich coastline brings it to a proud 3,800 km/2,360 mi in length. Sandy beaches, lined by pine forests, rugged limestone cliffs and deserted islands. A complete work of art of Baltic coastal nature. What a contrast to the capital. Cobblestone alleys, lined by top gabled merchants' houses and Gothic church towers that scrape the summer sky: Tallinn can claim to be one of the most beautiful Old Towns in Europe, Hanseatic-medieval influenced and superbly restored. The Grey Soviet muff has given way to a mix of elegant shops, restaurants and trendy cafés, and if it is a bit ordinary, you can use your mobile phone to pay the parking metre, city bus and movie ticket. Tallinn is Estonia's head and heart. Beyond the capital, life is much more leisurely. But there is one thing in this placid country that you will find in even the smallest village, internet for free. The blue-white signs with the @ symbol are so typically ethnic, just as the singing festivals and the cornflowers in May.

Where the Baltic Sea is called the "Western Sea": Estonia fascinates with Nordic nature, beaches and a Hanseatic influenced capital

TALLINN

Tallinn is Estonia's pride and joy – a lively waft of Scandinavian flair blows through it; it also still seems very much like a Hanseatic metropolis (pop. 400,000).

In the winding streets of the former Reval, visitors stroll through an open-air museum of historical architecture and look at the meticulously restored facades of Gothic merchants' houses, the gables, the towers, the fortified walls. 700 years of architectural history: enough reason to elevate the whole Vanalinn Old Town to Unesco World Heritage status. Vanalinn is divided into two. The Domberg (Toompea) in the southwest is the original city centre. The aristocracy and the clergy once lived here around the old Ordensburg and the cathedral, and in a manner of speaking looked down on the Hanseatic merchants and craftsmen in the lower part of town – and each part still has its own unique character.

SIGHTSEEING

DOMBERG (TOOMPEA) ⭐ (*11/A3*)

Originally, and old Estonian settlement was situated here. Then the Danes and after them the German knights built a castle on it. The mountain's most important attraction is the Long Hermann (Pikk Hermann), the largest preserved tower of the old castle (13th century). Sections of the structure were used to build the castle of Catherine II, which houses the Estonian Parliament *(Riigikogu | Lossi plats 1 a)* today. Opposite is the Orthodox Alexander Nevsky Cathedral *(Alexander-Nevski-katedraal | daily 8am–7pm)* from the tsarist era. The 13th century cathedral *(Toom Kirik | Tue–Sun 9am–4pm Toomkooli 6)* is even older, and one of the earliest churches in Estonia.

THREE SISTERS (KOLMÕDE) (*11/B2*)

The sisters are three of the most beautiful medieval building examples in Estonia's capital. Like all medieval merchants' houses, they served as homes and warehouses at the same time. The group of buildings that arose in Tallinn during the first half of the 15th century is the counterpart of the "Three Brothers" in Rīga. The arched top windows were fitted later. *Pikk 71*

GUILD HOUSES (*11/B3*)

Magnificent guild houses bear witness to the wealth and power of the merchants during the medieval period. Two buildings are still preserved: the *Great Guild (Suurgildi hoone | Pikk 17)* from 1410 once served as the clubhouse of the powerful merchant organisation. Today it is a museum. In the *House of the Blackheads (Mustpeade vennaskonna maja) | Pikk 26)*, the single merchants gathered.

KATHARINENTAL (KADRIORG)

The Baroque Palace, Katherinental, was built for Tsar Peter I in 1718–36 and is an architectural gem of Tallinn. The extensive palace complex houses three museums, one of these is the branch of the *art museum Kadriorgu Kunstimuuseum (Tue–Sun 10am–5pm | Weizenbergi 37 | www.ekm.ee/en)* Estonia's president resides on the former office building. The flower and palace garden invites you to stroll.

KUMU ART MUSEUM (EESTI KUNSTIMUUSEUM) ⭐ ✿

Kumu is the hotspot of Tallinn's cultural landscape. Externally, the futuristic acuteangled building, by the Finn Pekka Vapaavuori, already attracts people. Behind the limestone façade, the art museum has seven floors and 15,000 m²/18,000 yd² of

SUN, SAND AND SEA

Tallinn is situated at the sea. But ironically the coasts – and most of the islands – were a military restricted area for many centuries. The fear of the Soviets was great, the people could escape via the sea route or over ice in the winter. Today the Tallinn residents mostly spend their free time at the sea. The construction of the coastal promenade was certainly lengthy. But the Pirita and Viimsi beaches (just beyond the town) are the destinations of half of the town during summer weekends. The natureloving Tallinn locals also seek the coasts during the winter, for walking and crosscountry skiing.

Harmoniously landscaped gardens in front of the Katharinental Palace

the biggest art collection of the Baltic Sea – nearly 60,000 images, graphic works, sculptures and prints. *Kumu* is on the edge of Kadriorg's city park, near the presidential palace. *May–Sept Tue–Sun 10am–5pm | Wheat Bergi 37 | www.ekm.ee/en*

MARITIME MUSEUM/SEAPLANE HARBOUR (EESTI MEREMUUSEUM/ LENNUSADAM) *(*⊠ *11/A1)*

The location of this unique museum in the Baltic region is worth discovering: it is part of the Estonian Maritime Museum, in the old hangars of the Tallinn Seaplane Harbour from the tsarist period.

The huge premises (6500 m²/7800 yd²) feature historic aircraft and ships, including the wreckage of a cargo sailer from the 16th century, and the U-boat "Lembit" that was built in 1937 – the 600-ton colossus is the oldest fully functional warship after its retirement in 2011. On the reconstructed icebreaker, *Suur Tõll*, the ship's cook dishes up the **INSIDER TIP** same meals served to the crew a hundred years ago. With café and summer terrace. *Tue–Sun 10am–7pm | Vesilennuki tee 6 | www. lennusadam.eu*

ST. NICHOLAS' CHURCH (NIGULISTE KIRIK) *(*⊠ *11/B3)*

The late Gothic building (13th century) was financed by Dutch merchants who had settled in Tallinn. The church dominates this part of the Old Town and was not only a church, but also served as a safe hiding place for valuable merchandise. Today it houses an exhibition of medieval crafts. *Wed–Sun 10am–5pm | Niguliste 3 | Tours in English, can be booked on Tel. 6 44 99 03 | www.ekm.ee/en*

TOWN HALL, TOWN HALL SQUARE (RAEKODA, RAEKOJA PLATS) *(*⊠ *11/B3)*

Just like it was back then, the Town Hall is the meeting place of town life today. Festivals take place during the summer, cafés set up tables outside. The Town Hall itself is the only surviving Gothic Town Hall (1402) of the Baltic region. At the top of the octagonal tower on the east side,

BERTH

▶ **TALLINN**
In Tallinn, cruise ships are quite central, about 15 minutes from the city centre by foot.

the *Old Thomas*, a weather vane guards the city. A visit to the magnificent interior from the Hanseatic period is worthwhile. The Old Pharmacy *(Raekoja Plats 11)* is also worth a visit.

TOWN WALL (LINNA MÜÜR) ☀
(📖 11/B3)
From the 13th century, the lower town within the castle fortification was integrated into the Domberg, the wall was expanded for that. When completed, it was one of the greatest strongholds of medieval times in North Europe: 3m thick, 16m high and 46 defence towers. A good half of the structure has been preserved and is accessible in many

Tallinn's medieval fortification

places *(Nunne–St)*. Towers worth seeing: *Kiek in de Kök (peek in the kitchen) | Maiden's Tower (Neitsitorn) | Fat Margaret with maritime museum. (Wed–Sun 10am–6pm).*
The small, hidden place **INSIDER TIP** ▶ *Lühike jalg*, within the old town fortification and close to the Maiden's Tower, is one of Tallinn's most romantic places and a meeting place for young people.

SHOPPING

The main shopping street of modern Tallinn is the *Viru*. You can find the largest range of fashion labels at the chic shopping mecca, *Viru Keskus (daily 9am–9pm) | Viru väljak 4/6 or Gonsiori 2 | www.viruskeskus.com)*, which almost immediately swallowed the traditional store *Kaubamaja*. Otherwise, you run into one handicraft shop *(Käsitöö)* after the other in the touristically prepared Old Town.

WHERE TO GO

LAHEMA NATIONAL PARK ★
The largest and oldest national park in Estonia covers the most beautiful part of the rugged north coast, from which the four large peninsulas, Pärispea, Käsmu, Vergi and Juminda, extend into the Baltic Sea. In the interior there are deep pine forests, upland moors, rivers and 14 lakes. Lahema also houses some of the finest Baltic German ensembles in Estonia. Palmse Manor is the most popular, where the national park's visitors' centre is also situated *(Laheema rahvuspargi looduskeskus | daily 9am–5pm | www.lahemaa.ee)* The Sagadi Manor is equally worth seeing; it houses a Forest Museum *(daily 10am–4pm, entrance 3 euros | Sagadi mõis | www.sagadi.ee)*.

TRAVEL TIPS

The Baltic region: the most important information for your trip

EMERGENCY NUMBERS

Estonia: *fire brigade/ambulance 112, police 110*. Latvia and Lithuania: *central emergency number 112* (also from mobile)

HEALTH

The European Health Insurance Card (EHIC) is also valid in the Baltic region. Swiss people are also entitled to the same treatment as at home. However, prepayment is required. Taking out foreign health insurance is recommended. Most medicines are available over the counter in pharmacies. If you are planning hikes in nature, you should get vaccinated against tick bites (TBE) before you travel, and take good mosquito repellent for outdoor trips.

INTERNET & WIFI

In many cities you can now access the internet for free via WiFi. Estonia practically has an extensive, stable and fast WiFi network. There are almost 1,200 hotspots, recognisable by the orange and black Wi-Fi symbols. For a complete overview of all hotspot locations, including the free ones: *www.WiFi.ee*. Even in remote villages there are @ signs that indicate the public internet access. In Lithuania and Latvia, WiFi is limited to larger cities and tourist centres.

MONEY & CREDIT CARDS

Most banks in the Baltic region accept the usual credit and debit cards. ATMs (Visa, Eurocard, EC) are also widespread throughout the country. Banks are usually open from Mon–Fri 9am–6pm, some also on Saturdays. In the capitals you can pay by credit card almost everywhere.

TOILETS

In the Baltic region, something as simple as going to the toilet can be guesswork, since you can't rely on the Western European symbolism here. For toilet signs, the following symbols are often used: Δ = Women, $\blacktriangledown$ = Men. Take note: in Estonian the "m" stands for *mees* = man. In Lithuanian the "m" stands for *moterys* = women! When you are in Estonia, "n" means woman, m means man. In Lithuanian m = women, v = man.

BUDGETING

Coffee	£1.4/$1.6
	1 cup of coffee
Beer	£1.6/$1.9
	0.5 l local brand
Snack	£2.7/$3.3
	for a Kiev chop
Sauna	£11-18/$13-22
	for 2 hours

RUSSIA

Russia is a land of contrasts. Palm trees stretch into the sky along the southern beach promenades, while icy polar winds cause the thermometer to drop below minus 50 degrees Celsius in the north.

In Kamchatka in the far east, volcanoes rise and challenge adventurers, while the Baltic coast, the western point of the country relies on amber extraction. The splendid St. Petersburg is also situated here, though it is only the "second capital" (as it is often colloquially referred to) after Moscow. Moscow is everything, the economic capital and the home of the political elite. Russia is not only contrast-rich, but also enormous: the distance between the coasts of the Baltic Sea and the Chukchi Sea in the far east measures nearly 10,000 km/6,215 mi and the territory of the country covers nine time zones; at the Baltic coast you don't need to convert the time too much.

ST. PETERS-BURG

The St. Petersburg Old Town, which was built before the 1917 revolution, is huge – about 6 km/3.7 mi both from north to south and from east to west. Luckily, the concrete buildings at the World Heritage-listed city ensemble was left untouched, and the damage

A real pearl of Russia is situated on the Baltic Sea coast: St. Petersburg enchants with opulent splendour

caused by the siege in the Second World War has been carefully repaired. Top-class museums, palaces, magnificent buildings, cathedrals, monasteries and magnificent squares are distributed throughout this heritage area in huge numbers. Great distances have to be covered during a city tour! Not only the inner city is appealing, you should visit at least one of the splendid palaces of the tsars outside the city, for example the Catherine Palace in 30 km/19 mi distance.

BRONZE HORSEMAN (MEDNY WSADNIK) ★ (*12/B3*)

St. Petersburg's most popular landmark. The imposing monument displays the city founder as a dynamic visionary, who heads forward on his rearing horse with a big jump. The work of the Frenchman Etienne Falconet, on the Senate Square, would have been only half as attractive if it did not stand on the thick wave-shaped pedestal. It was created from an approx-

SHOPPING

Between art and kitsch: when shopping you'll find Russian dolls and fur caps

Bargains are rare, because boutiques and shopping centres in the city centre are glamorous. Russian goods are not expensive at all – and can hardly be found at home: designer fashion, bags, watches, scarves, hats, caps...

The *Nevsky Prospect* is and remains the most important shopping street – even though it is next to the area around the Gostiny Dvor, between the square and Moscow train station where the *Galeria* and the *Nevsky Centre* shopping malls

LOW BUDGET

Not in the mood for Nevsky glamour? The *Pik* and *Sennaya* shopping centres at the Haymarket *(Metro 2,4,5 Sennaja Ploschtschad/Sadowaja/ Spasskaja)* allow for everyday shopping at normal prices, as well as malls and hypermarkets at the *Akademitscheskaja (line 1), Ladoshskaja (line 4), Meshdunarodnaja (line 5)* or *Kuptschino (line 2)* metro stations.

are, it has developed into a new consumer magnet.

The liberal opening hours are customer-friendly: shops open between 9 and 11am and remain open till 7 or 10 pm, without lunch break. On Sundays – except for some speciality shops – almost all stores are open, although not always as long as on weekdays. The lively markets are also open daily from about 9am to 7pm. And many supermarkets, but also smaller grocery shops and even some pharmacies and bookshops, are open around the clock. However, alcohol may not be sold from 10pm to 11am. It is not hard to find classic Russian souvenirs in the city centre, like vodka, fur caps, amber jewellery and of course the (currently very fake) Russian dolls, but also real handicrafts, such as filigree painted lacquer tins, porcelain figurines or carvings made of birch bark. In a cultural metropolis like Petersburg is also worthwhile to be on the lookout for work by local artists.

imately 1,600-ton rock, which was located 12 km/7.5 mi away. For it to be transported, a catamaran was built from two sailing ships. The name "Bronze Horseman" was taken from a poem by Pushkin in 1833. In Russian the monument is called "Copper Horseman" – even though it is a bronze statue. *Senatskaja Ploschtschad | Metro 5 Admiraltejskaia*

CHURCH OF THE RESURRECTION OF CHRIST (SPAS NA KROWI) ★ (🛱 12/B3)

This colourful onion-shaped tower church is out of the ordinary in St. Petersburg's cityscape: it was only built in 1887-1907, in traditional neo-Russian style. The reason for the construction was the anarchist assassination attempt on Tsar Alexander II, who was killed here in 1881 by a bomb. Inside, a shrine was erected over the spot of the pavement where the tsar was mortally wounded. The colour orgy of the enamel domes continues here: the walls of this huge jewellery box are completely lined with mosaics – a total of 7,000m² | *Information and opening times at www. cathedral.ru*

GOLITSYN LOFT ★ (🛱 12/B4)

Not only attractive because of architecture and history. Even though it is a romantic old town palace from 1790 on the Fontanka, where Pushkin used to visit Count Golitsyn, the highlight is its current utilisation: in 2016 about five dozen creative small businesses moved in – and now breathe new life into the old walls around the courtyard, which is used to stage events. Only absolutely necessary renovation is being done. For a little money you can eat well here, enjoy original drinks, relax, celebrate, babble, dance, vape or smoke hookahs, sunbathe on the balcony, spend the night, buy art, clothes or accessories, get a new hairstyle or a tattoo – in short, immerse yourself intensely in the colourful scene of the largest creative cluster in St. Petersburg. Go, look, hang around where you like! Individual opening hours, not much is happening before noon | *Naberezhnaja reki Fontanki 20 | www.luna-info. ru/spaces | Tram 3 | Bus 46,49*

HERMITAGE (GOSUDARSTVENNY ERMITASH) ★ (🛱 12/C3)

For artists, the Hermitage is reason enough to come to Petersburg, because this overwhelming museum is right on par with the Louvre, Prado or the "Met" in New York. However, the Hermitage is far more than just a museum rich in world-class cultural treasures: the Winter Palace and its additions, the former main residence of the tsar dynasty are themselves the most magnificent of the 60,000 exhibits on display. For those who only enjoy the historical aura and wish to marvel at the wealth of Russia's rulers, it is

Impressive: the castle bridge

also easy to simply wander aimlessly and informally through the labyrinth of rooms and apartments.

Visitors enter the wide courtyard of the Winter Palace from the castle square through a magnificent gate. This Baroque castle with over 1000 rooms was built in 1754–62 by Francesco Rastrelli, "to the glory of Russia". *Information and opening hours at www.hermitage.ru*

ST. ISAAC'S CATHEDRAL (ISSAKIJEWS-KI SOBOR) ★ (📖 12/B4)

With a height of 101 metres, the cathedral dominates the city centre – the golden church dome is the fourth largest in the world. The St. Petersburgers fondly give the sacred building further superlatives: there is space for 12,000 people, it rests on 10,762 piles. The walls are up to 5m thick. For the gold coating, 400kg of gold was used. 43 different minerals were used for the lavish design of the interior. Externally, with its 112 monolithic columns of Karelian granite it projects strength and rigidity; inside it is bright and festive. The central element is the white marble iconostasis, flanked by malachite and lazurite columns. 300 sculptures and 150 paintings make the cathedral what it officially is today: a museum in which *services* are also held *(Sat from 4pm, Sun from 10am)*. You should not miss the ⬆ colonnade of the cathedral: from 40m high, it offers a wonderful panoramic view. St. *Isaac's Square* is right at your feet. In the centre is the *equestrian monument*, since 1859, designed by Montferrand for *Tsar Nicholas I*. He succeeded in balancing the 6m high sculpture created by Peter Klodt so that it stands only on the hind legs of the horse. Beyond the Blue Bridge over the Moika, the Mariinsky Palace (1839-44) rises, now the seat of the city parliament. *Information and opening times at: www.cathedral.ru | Metro 5 Admiraltejskaia*

PALACE BRIDGE (DWORZOWY MOST) (📖 12/B-C3)

The Palace Bridge is undoubtedly one of the most famous sights of St. Petersburg and is literally unmissable. Built in 1912–16, next to the Winter Palace, the Neva crossing magically attracts the public during white nights: its raised wings in front of the silhouette of the Peter and Paul Fortress and the pastel

TWO CLASSES AT THE CASH REGISTERS

An unpleasant legacy from long-gone Soviet time is the price policy of some museums, which include the Hermitage, Peterhof and Pavlovsk tsar castles and the Mariinsky Theatre: foreigners have to pay 20 to 120 percent more admission than local visitors. The cultural institute justifies this with the income disparities and the fact that the Russians already finance the tourism attractions with their tax money. Objecting does not help much, and only those who really speak Russian perfectly can try to cheat. There is some consolation: in the 1990s, the price difference was significantly greater.

Outside and inside, art of the highest quality: the Hermitage

sky are Petersburg's motif par excellence. Especially during the weekends, a boozy street party rages here with all sorts of jugglers. The municipality contributes to this and plays classical music by Russian composers at the open bridge from June to August. *April–Nov daily open during these times: 1:10–2:50pm 3:10–4:55pm | Metro 5 Admiraltejskaia*

PUBS

BEER FAMILY

Due to the stucco ceiling alone, this is definitely not a pub – but a club-like restaurant for beer lovers: 30 varieties on tap and 400 from the glass refrigerator. The ☀ INSIDERTIP porch high above the sidewalk, is unique to the whole Nevsky. *Nevsky Prospekt 47 | Metro 3 Mayakovskaya*

DICKENS ★

Despite (or because of?) the luxurious Victorian style, this large pub – it offers 40 different beers! – attracts a colourful audience. In summer there is a small beer garden on the Fontanka shore. *Nabarezhnaya reki Fontanki 108 | Metro 1,2 Technological Institute*

INSIDERTIP TOLSTY FRAJER

Original pub chain with Soviet atmosphere: but the agitation posters, slogans and appeals to the comrades are not displayed aggressively, but ironically transformed into a pleasant design. With beer, a plate of snacks is served for free, but the menu is also worthy of a restaurant. One problem: it is often too full – also because of the democratic prices. *Uliza Belinskogo 13; Uliza Dumskaja 3; Uliza mira 11; W.O. | 8. Linie 43*

FOOD & DRINK

Exotic competitors for *bliny* and *borscht*: the gastronomy exudes international flair

Pizza and pasta, bratwurst, Asian food from the wok, exquisite Mediterranean cuisine – St. Petersburg's food is as varied as it is international. Beyond that, it is amazingly modern and creative, because the gastronomy industry effectively started from scratch in 1991, after the end of the depressing Soviet years.
But that does not mean that the Russians stopped loving the most hearty, traditional dishes of their local cuisine. On the contrary, they stick to their eating habits: big nutritious soup portions, an enormous variety of *zakuski* (appetisers), the love of mushrooms – and vodka is always an alternative to (expensive) wine. Locals also enjoy the Georgian cuisine, which has enriched Russia's cuisine with Mediterranean spices and sophisticated grill techniques. Not to mention the Caucasian hospitality: a stop at a Georgian restaurant is simply a must in St. Petersburg.
The customary names are a bit confusing: a kafe is a small restaurant with quite an extensive offer. When you want coffee or cake, a *kofejnja* or *konditorskaja* is the right place. A restoran is for those who would like to experience cuisine and service of a higher standard. This also means that there is live music at night, then people can even dance. A bar is either a tavern or a bar – normally also with detailed menu and an ample assortment of beers. Because the craft beer boom has also reached Russia.

LOCAL SPECIALITIES

Beef stroganoff – named after a noble dynasty: sliced beef fillet in a sauce of onions, sour cream and mushrooms
Bliny – pancakes made with buckwheat flour, usually stuffed with mushrooms or minced meat, little buckwheat cakes are called oladji
Borscht – deep red soup from beetroot, white cabbage and beef, often with tomato puree, potatoes, onions – and smetana (sour cream)

TRAVEL TIPS

St. Petersburg: the most important information for your trip

BERTH

▶ ST. PETERSBURG

Cruise ships dock at the modern Marine Façade Harbour, about 5 km/3 mi from the centre.

CLIMATE

The weather in St. Petersburg is latently unstable, humid and cool. From early June till mid-July, the white nights in Petersburg are especially attractive (and overcrowded). But in May and August the evenings are also very long and the light is hardly different. September and October are pleasant months, especially in the autumnal castle parks. There is no guarantee of snow during the winter – but it can be white between the end of October and mid-April!

CUSTOMS

With regard to art works and antiques: anything older than 100 years old may not be exported, younger objects with "considerable cultural value" are also off limits. Usual souvenirs and smaller contemporary pictures (keep the receipt!), can be exported without problems. The EU grants duty-free imports of a maximum of 200 cigarettes, 1 l of spirits and 125g sturgeon caviar. You can import and export foreign currency up to USD 10,000 (or equivalent) without declaring it. And you can export foreign currency up to USD 3,000 (or equivalent) without declaring it.

MONEY & CREDIT CARDS

The rouble is freely convertible. Paying in dollars or pounds is prohibited! Roubles can be bought at the increasingly rare bureaux de change (obmen valuty) – for amounts from 40,000 Rbl, a passport must be presented – or at good rates with credit or Eurocheque cards at ATMs (auto tellers), in shopping centres and metro entrances. In comparison with Germany, modes of transport, basic foodstuffs and cigarettes are significantly cheaper. The same applies to the UK. Branded products and electronic devices are usually 10 to 30 percent more expensive.

SAFETY

Petersburg is a safe place – with an exception: especially in buses, the metro and in busy cafés, the risk of pickpocketing is very high. In this regard extreme caution and alertness are required. Rather leave your passport on the ship – and put a copy of the data page and visa in your pocket. Otherwise, the occasional very high kerbstones are the most dangerous in St. Petersburg!

TIME ZONE

Moscow time zone. In 2011, Russia abolished winter time. Therefore, in the summer it is CEST + 2 hours, in the winter CET + 3 hours.

FINLAND

Finland is often called "the land of the thousand lakes" – but that is an understatement. If you come here, you can look forward to nearly 187,888 lakes, 3.2 million saunas and sheer endless forests.

The landscape looks like a patchwork carpet of blue and green. In between are red wooden cottages with white window frames. These typical Finnish log cabins with saunas and Bullerbyn charm are called mökkis in Finnish and are a dream for nature lovers. Here there is no rush, no stress, no noise: two weeks at the lake is holiday for the soul. For those who seek for a change in the meantime: visit your neighbours: the Finns know how to celebrate summer. Only 5.4 million people live in Suomi, as the country is called in Finnish. Their lifestyle is influenced by a short summer in which life explodes. Anyone who travels through the country around mid-summer – around 21 June – notes that no one sleeps, everyone celebrates.

HELSINKI

The Finnish capital, Helsinki (pop. 620,700) is a small, vibrant world metropolis. With all the bustle of a big town, it exudes peace and friendly serenity.

The urban core, an architectural jewel of past stylistic periods, rests on granite peninsulas directly at the sea. When you arrive by ship you will see the white cathedral and the golden domes of the Uspen-

Photo: Finland's desolate natural beauty

Finland is a country full of variety, with untouched landscapes, thousands of islands and the charming metropolis of Helsinki

ski Cathedral as you enter the Suomenlinna fortress, where fish, vegetables, souvenirs and specialities are sold at the market square. The Esplanadi boulevard leads from here to the centre and is a meeting place and promenade. Ice cream stands sell huge scoops, fine stores sell international fashion, cafés serve berry pies. Street musicians, businesswomen, dockworkers, families – when the sun shines everyone enjoys the light, Mediterranean-like atmosphere. All major attractions can be reached on foot, by bicycle or by tram

(2 and 3) – the city's beloved cultural asset. The change from the city into nature is easy. Helsinki, the beautiful "daughter of the Baltic Sea", is blessed with sandy beaches and coastal islands, further inland, a cultivated landscape invite you to take a trip.

SIGHTSEEING

ESPLANADI ★ *(🛱 13/C2)*
On the green promenade between the magnificent facades of the main shop-

ping streets, *Phojois-* and *Etelä-Esplanadi*, you will find fine shops, Hotel Kämp, cafés and benches. The bronze statue *Havis Amanda* created by Ville Valgren in 1908, stands at the east end. The naked maiden is a symbol of the city and was highly controversial when it was unveiled. Today she receives a student cap each year on 1 May.

FOUNTAIN PARK (KAIVOPUISTO) ☆ *(ᗰ 13/C-D4)*

The large park in the embassy district in the southeast of the city is located directly at the sea, in the similarly named district, Kaivopuisto, and was designed as a spa resort in 1830. From the rocks at the Ursa observatory, which was built in 1926, you can enjoy beautiful views of islands and marinas. The club restaurant *Kaivohuone* is a top address for elegant night owls in summer.

At the beach promenade, *Merisatama-ranta*, people meet for ice cream, to chill or to wash carpets at **INSIDER TIP** *Mattolaituri* (*Moderate*).

ISLANDS

If you want to escape the big city, an island is always accessible. Here you will find peace, beaches, walking paths, well-kept restaurants. The most popular island (5 km/3 mi northwest of the centre) is ★ *Seurasaari*. A wooden bridge connects it with the mainland. The main attraction is the *open-air museum (June–Aug daily 11am–5pm | 8 euros | bus 24 from the centre)*. Historic buildings from all parts of Finland are here, including old farm houses and a little wooden church. Concerts and festivals frequently take place on Seurasaari. On the weekend after 21 June, the Midsummer Festival is celebrated with dance, music and Helsinki's biggest *midsummer bonfire* is celebrated.

KIASMA (MUSEUM OF CONTEMPORARY ART) *(ᗰ 13/B2)*

The name Kiasma (crossing) refers to the futuristic architecture of the museum with its round aluminium-and-glass construction. The building displays contemporary art of mainly Finnish and Scandinavian artists. *Tue 10am–5pm, Wed–Fri 10am–8:30pm, Sat/Sun 10am–6pm | 10 euros, free entrance for under 18s | Mannerheiminaukio 2*

KRUUNUNHAKA *(ᗰ 13/C2)*

The oldest part of the city, behind the cathedral, impresses with Art Nouveau

KALEVALA

The national epic, Kalevala, is a collection of ancient legends and myths that have been passed on to the people through song for centuries. Elias Lönnrot (1802–84) wandered through Finland for 20 years to write down a thousand verse lines, probably anticipating that the tradition of oral tradition would become extinct at the end of the 19th century. The first issue appeared in 1835 and has strongly influenced the Finnish national consciousness. The epic is still alive today and inspires average Finns such as artists. It has been translated into numerous languages. The light, straightforward comic version by Mauri Kunnas is available in every bookshop.

Helsinki's Nordic beauty unfolds in the water

buildings; the oldest wooden house, the *Ruiskumestarin talo (Kristianinkatu 12)* from 1818 stands here. From the eastern shore you can reach the Tar Island and the Smoke restaurant, *Savu (daily | Tervasaarenkannas 3 | Tel. 09 74 25 55)*

NATIONAL MUSEUM (KANSALLISMUSEO) *(13/B1)*
The domed hall of the National Romantic granite building from 1916 is adorned with frescoes by the painter Akseli Gallen with motifs from the national epic, Kalevala. Finnish history from the Stone Age till today is exhibited. *Tue–Sun 11am–6pm | 9 euros | Mannerheimintie 34*

ROCK CHURCH (TEMPPELIAUKION KIRKKO) *(13/A–B2)*
The underground church from 1969 was excavated directly into granite according to the design by the architect brothers, Timo and Tuomo Suomalainen. Rock walls support a huge dome of copper strands and glass. The space is appreciated best by attending a concert or a service. *Mon–Fri 9:30am–5pm, Sat/Sun irregular | entrance free | Lutherinkatu 3 | Töölö*

SENATE SQUARE (SENAATINTORI) ★ *(13/C2)*
The square is considered one of the greatest examples of the neoclassical architectural style. Tsar Alexander I had the government district of his new Finnish capital built according to plans by C. L. Engel (1816–52). A mighty staircase leads up to the towering white cathedral, *Tuomiokirkko*, from 1852 (daily 9am–6pm, June–Aug till midnight). From the *cathedral terrace* there is a stunning view of the square with the government palace, university and the statue of Alexander II.

SUOMENLINNA ★
Only 15 minutes by ferry and you will reach the fortress islands of Suomenlinna,

TRAVEL WITH KIDS

KORKEASAARI ZOO
The zoo's 150 fascinating wildlife species, including the endangered Amur Leopard, live idyllically on a large island near Helsinki. *Daily from 10am | Adults 12 euros, children 6–17 years 6 euros, with paddle steamer from Kauppatori 18/9 euros | Korkeasaari Island | www.korkeasaari.fi*

the "Finnish Castle". The facility was supposed to be a fortress against Russia – in vain. In 1809 Finland came under Russian rule, and the fortress became a Russian garrison town. Today it is a World Heritage site and excursion destination. A visitor centre and six museums provide information about the history *(daily from 10am | 6 euros). Crossing with HKL ferry*

Finnish house idyll in Porvoo

(local transport ticket is valid), from Kauppatori, 3 times every hour

FOOD & DRINK

INSIDER TIP BLINIT
Just like in St. Petersburg: filled pancakes and Russian cuisine in overdrive, delicious, cheap and with a satiety guarantee. *Mon closed | Sturenkatu 9 | Te. 0400 90 96 03 | Budget*

JUURI ●
Have you ever tried *sapas*? The Finnish variety of tapas is made from local ingredients – like many other dishes. Juuri means "root" – back to the Finnish roots, that is the concept. The attached shop, i.a., sells cheese, sausage, vegetables and handmade products from the region. *Daily | Korkeavuorenkatu 27 | Tel. 09 63 57 32 | www.juuri.fi | Moderate*

WHERE TO GO

ESPOO
The second biggest town in Finland (pop. 265,000) is situated between forests, meadows, lakes and sea. The Nuuksio National Park and Haltia Nature Centre *(Nuuksiontie 84 | www.haltia.com)* are also part of Espoo. The summer restaurant **INSIDER TIP** *Gula Villan (info and opening times at: www.gulavillan.fi | Bus 132 from Kamppi till Nokkala, info about ferry boats: short.travel/fin9)* radiates island charm.

PORVOO ★
Wooden houses nestle picturesquely on the slope of the river valley, red warehouses line the shore. Museums, cafés, art galleries and small shops are hidden in windy backyards. Porvoo has inspired many important artists for centuries, and there is still an artists' colony today.

SHOPPING

Elk salami or birch wood crafts are typical Finnish souvenirs

Finland is a combination of village shops and *American Dream:* family markets and market halls selling fresh natural products and US-style shopping centres co-exist. The biggest "village shop" in Finland is a mixture of both, with 6 million visitors a year: *Tuuri kyläkauppa (at Ätäri | www.tuuri.fi)*. But above all, almost everything is online: *www.suomikauppa.fi*

BOOKS & CDS

Music CDs and photo books are nice souvenirs, as well as comics by Mauri Kunnas. The *Academic Bookstore (Pohjoisesesplandi 39)* in Helsinki keeps English editions of Finnish books.

DELICACIES AND COSMETICS

Good culinary souvenirs are elk salami, reindeer ham, smoked salmon and marinated fish. Furthermore, wine, liqueur (all suppliers: *www.viinitlat.net*), berry marmalade as well as chocolate and liquorice. Natural soaps with essential oils from Aamumaa, *Flowkosmetiikka* or *Solavoima*, are in demand. A hand towel, tar shampoo, pine fragrance and a felt sauna cap for sauna fans. Practical and a hit in the country: xylitol chewing gun, which active ingredient is extracted from birch sap. it tastes sweet and is said to protect against tooth decay.

TEXTILES

Marimekko (Kämp Gallery | Phojoisesplanadi 33 | Helsinki) not only makes fashion, but also supplies things like pot holders or umbrellas with a mix of large-scale patterns and flashy colours. In the design district of Helsinki, you can also find Anniki Karvinen, Samuji, Ivana and shoe designer Minna Parikka. Gloves and hats made with felt are warm, beautiful and durable *(www.feltaction.fi);* the felt fashion of *www.sipuseiska.fi* is high quality and original. Hand-woven carpets, linen towels, sweaters, local fur and bobbin lace from Rauma are traditional.

The Pommern museum ship is situated in Mariehamn

MARIEHAMN/ ÅLAND- ISLANDS

The islanders speak only Swedish, even though they belong to Finland. The ⭐ **Åland Islands lie between the two Nordic countries in the Gulf of Bothnia.**

Sandy beaches and straits, a mild marine climate and storm-tossed coasts, biodiverse nature and the omnipresent water characterise the landscape of the 6,500 islands, on which there is only one town: *Maryam* (pop. 11,000) was established in 1861 and becomes a bustling entertainment metropolis in the summer. The ferry traffic which connects most of the 60 inhabited islands also contributes to this – with more than 1.5 million visitors to Maryam per year, most of them are Swedish. Swedish is also the official language of the region. The League of Nations decided in 1921 that Åland indeed belonged to Finland, but that it could manage its own affairs. The reason why the predominant language is Swedish is that these islands were part of Sweden for many centuries. As a sign of its autonomy, Åland has its own flag and stamps. Since 1854 the region has also been demilitarised.

SIGHTSEEING

BOMARSUND FORTRESS RUINS ⚜
The remains of the Russian fortress are freely accessible and offer beautiful views of the surrounding area. Planned as a strategic control point to control the Baltic Sea region, it was still incomplete during the Crimean War in 1854, and it was destroyed soon afterwards. *www.bomarsund.ax*

CHURCHES
Åland has 15 medieval fieldstone churches with beautiful towers. The

oldest stone building in Finland is the church in *Jomala* (1270). In *Lemland* and *Sund*, the oldest murals on limestone can be seen. The wooden sculptures in *Finström* date back to the 12th century. The other churches are in *Eckerö, Föglö, Geta, Hammarland, Kumlinge, Saltvik* and *Vardö* – translated, the name means "Guardian Island", and is a reminder of bygone times, when Vardö was a stopover on the postal route from Turku to Stockholm.

KASTELHOLMS CASTLE ★

The castle from the 14th century is Åland's most visited attraction. In its heyday, it was the foothold of the Swedish crown. After raids and fires, not much of its old splendour was left over, except for ruins, but efforts have been made for more than 30 years to reconstruct the castle. Surrounded by moats, it stands out in a picturesque landscape. The *Vita Björn prison museum* and the Jan Karls*gården open-air museum* are attached *(May–Sept Daily 10am–5pm | Entrance free)*. Here midsummer celebrations are a colourful event: the Johannus tree is traditionally decorated and dancing and singing continue till late at night. In the middle of July there is also a medieval market during the *Gustav Vasa days*. *July daily 10am–6pm, May–mid Sept 10am–5pm | 6 euros | Sund www.kastelholm.ax*

MUSEUM SHIP POMMERN

The last preserved four-masted barque in its original state is moored in the western harbour of Mariehamn. The "Queen of sailing ships" was built in 1903 and was used as a grain transporter between Australia and England as well as Denmark. She retired in 1939 and the Pommern has been a museum ship since 1953. On board there is a recommended exhibition and a documentary about life at sea. *June–Aug daily, May/Sept 11am–4pm | 10 euros (including maritime museum) | sjofartsmuseum.ax*

SWEATING INSTEAD OF ARGUING

The Finnish sauna session is simple and close to nature, regardless if it is in a wooden house at a lake, at a camping place or rental apartment. There are no rules in Finland when it comes to sweating. It is permissible to do something that is good for you without bothering anyone. With the Juhannus festival, bundles of birch branches *(vihta)* are bound with which one beats oneself or another gently – it smells good and promotes the blood circulation. Offensive stares are out of place when sweating. Men and women mostly take saunas separately. On the other hand, there are numerous modifications of the sweatboxes: there is the sauna in the touring coach, RV trailer, as a mini electric version for an apartment and even in a gondola in Ylläs. The original smoke sauna *(savusauna)* is also experiencing a renaissance after almost going extinct due to frequent fires. If the infusion smells like tar, then there is *löylyterva* (sauna tar) in the infusion water, and besides vodka and cupping it is the third universal remedy of the old Finland.

FOOD & DRINK

Nature dishes up: Finnish cooks serve you the wilderness from forests and lakes

The traditional Finnish cuisine is nutritious and simple, aimed at getting a hard-working population through long, cold winters. Depending on the season, restaurants use fresh, typically Nordic products for their time-honoured recipes.

"Food fills you up", is what they say in Finland, and that is also how a lot of it tastes. The country's cuisine did not have a good reputation for cooking at five-star levels. But derogatory remarks expressed about Finnish cuisine by Silvio Berlusconi and Jacques Chirac have triggered a real *cooking boom*. Traditional ingredients such as beetroot, rutabaga and cabbage are being transformed into gourmet experiences with berries, fish and game. The selection of local fruits and vegetables is a bit sparse due to climatic conditions. But in the sparsely populated country, a lot of the produce is organic without certification: far away from industry and cities, fruits and vegetables grow with a *low level of pollution*, and game and fish naturally come from a species-appropriate altitude.

Even those who prefer traditional dishes and regional ingredients can now experience rewarding culinary adventures all over Finland. Helsinki is now favoured among gourmets. Stews, soups, casseroles, roasts and pies (dishes that are easy to prepare) still dominate everyday kitchen life.

LOCAL SPECIALITIES

Graavi lohi – pickled salmon with dill, available at every buffet and in supermarkets.

Jokiravut – in the summer it is crayfish season. The shellfish is served with white wine and toast.

Liekki lohi – flame-grilled salmon. The whole fish is opened, deboned, nailed to a grill and barbecued on an open fire.

Poronkäristys – sliced reindeer on mashed potato and cranberries.

Runenbergin torttu – the favourite tartletts of the national poet, Johan Ludvig Runeberg's. The filling consists of almonds and raspberry jam.

TRAVEL TIPS

Finland: the most important information for your trip

BERTHS

▶ HELSINKI
Large cruise ships dock at the West Harbour, about 4 km/2.5 mi from the centre.

▶ MARIEHAMN/ÅLAND-ISLANDS
In Mariehamn cruise ships dock very close to the centre.

CLIMATE

Finland has an eastern continental climate; this causes arctic cold temperatures in winter (down to -40 °C) and warm to hot days in the summer (up to 30 °C), so that the water temperature reaches 20 °C. It is rarely humid and in the evening it gets cold quickly. Due to the northern location, days are long and bright in the summer and short and dark in the winter. North of the Arctic Circle the midnight sun shines in the summer, in the winter, polar night with northern lights prevails. The peak tourism season in the summer is from mid-June till mid-August and the winter it is from early February till the end of April. Weather forecasts: *en.ilmatieteenlaitos.fi*

HEALTH

Finland ensures a high level of health care, also in the areas outside of the cities. Ask your health insurer how it settles with Finland, and take your European Health Insurance Card (EHIC) with you.

MONEY & CREDIT CARDS

The currency is the euro, card payments are common. Money can easily be drawn at ATMs with an EC card. You need to inform your bank that you'll be using your card in Europe. If you don't tell them, they'll probably put your account on hold because they'll assume the charges are fraudulent. There are exchange offices at airports, railway stations and in the big cities. Payments can also be made with mobiles/smart phones for bus and metro, parking machines or for shopping. Since all amounts in Finland are rounded to five cents, no one or two cent coins are in circulation. If you get your hands on these coins, keep them: this rare change is sought after by collectors.

TIME ZONE

The Eastern European time is one hour ahead of Central European time: set your clock one hour forward.

BUDGETING

Coffee	£2.7/$3.3
	for 1 cup
Sweets	£2/$2.4
	for 1 Fazer chocolate bar

SWEDEN

Bullerbyn and Lisbeth Salander! It is such contrasts that make up the almost 2,000 km/1,245 mi long country between Öresund and Northern Finland. And notwithstanding all the gloom and melancholy that was captured – not for the last time either – by the late master film director, Ingmar Bergan in his award-winning films, the Swedes are considered open, friendly and joyful. A little burdened by recent history, Sweden combines the best of yesterday with the best of tomorrow: unspoilt landscapes, cosy small towns, pristine waters and endless forests meet with high tech, innovative artists, a first-class infrastructure and open-minded people. Church members and conservative politicians also take part in the annual gay and lesbian pride festival in Stockholm, and paternity leave is the proper thing in the highest executive floors of the Wallenberg sphere. In the land of equality, with its long social democratic tradition, it is amazing that the royal family, especially Crown Princess Victoria enjoys unbelievable popularity.

STOCKHOLM

Tourist offices often exaggerate when they advertise their city. When it comes to Stockholm (pop. 950,000) the advertising slogan "beauty on water", is not sufficiently descriptive. Because apart from water, the beauty of Stockholm also has a lot of greenery to offer.

Photo: approaching Sweden from the water

Modern metropolises, top-class culture and spectacular landscapes – Sweden is a land of attractive contrasts

A third of Stockholm consists of water, a third is built-up area and one third green areas, and all three parts are equally worth seeing. In the summer, the Baltic Sea and Lake Mälaren invite you on boat excursions, in the winter you can go for a walk on ice or ice skate. You can hike in the parks any time of the year and afterwards you can relax at one of the cosy coffee shops and tea houses. Founded over 750 years ago, it consists of many islands, of which the historic Old Town, Gamla Stan, the for-

mer workers' quarter Södermalm and the exclusive district Östermalm are the best known. Stockholm is rich in museums – in addition to several art museums there are museums for music, theatre and toys. The city centre is relatively small and has a well-developed public transport network *(www.sl.se)*

SIGHTSEEING

An overview of current exhibitions, events, restaurants and shops can be

ISLAND EMPIRE

⭐ 30,000 small and large islands, barren rocks and green *archipelago paradise* extend 150 km/93 mi from north to south east of the city. For centuries people have lived here from fishing and agriculture. At the end of the19th century, the steamships created new revenue opportunities for the archipelago inhabitants, because city dwellers flocked out of the towns to summer resorts. Many rich people from Stockholm built splendid wooden villas on the islands, and the city of Stockholm bought properties and built simple structures, so that poorer families could enjoy the fresh air and unpolluted nature. In the 1950s and 1970s lucrative jobs attracted people to the city, and they left the area. An active archipelago policy finally stopped the downward trend and created new jobs. As before, the archipelago is a very popular destination in summer and winter. In addition to the more than 10,000 permanent residents, numerous holidaymakers spend their holidays on sailboats, in holiday houses, in the hotels, guest houses or hostels on the archipelago. Further information: *www.visitskargarden.se*

found on the internet at www.visitstockholm.com

ABBA – THE MUSEUM ⭐ (*🛍 14/F3*)
The most popular and successful Swedish pop band of all time has its own museum. Thanks to the latest technology, you can become the fifth band member and join in the fun. It is advisable to reserve tickets online for a specific time in high season. *May to August daily 10am–7pm | Entrance 250 SEK | Djurgårdsvägen 68 | www.abbathemuseum.com/en*

DJURGÅRDEN ⭐ (*🛍 14/F2–3*)
The former royal hunting grounds are a unique recreation island today with museums and a lot of greenery. *The Nordic Museum (daily 10am–5pm, Wed till 8pm | Entrance 120 SEK)* is located at the beginning of the island, with a collection of Nordic folklore as well as the newly renovated *Liljevalchs Konsthall (opening times and entrance fees on the website, unclear at the time of going to press | www.liljevalchs.se)* with alternating exhibitions of international artists. The 🌍 ecological garden, *Rosendals Trädgård (Feb–March and Nov/Dec Tue–Sun 11am–5pm, May–Sept daily 11am–5pm | www.rosendalstradgard.se)* and its café are also recommended. There you can also buy organic bread and homemade delicacies.

EKOPARKEN
The world's first urban national park is located in Stockholm and stretches over 10 km/6 mi through and around the city. Here, in the middle of the big city, hares, foxes and now and then even a moose say good night. Fifty clubs run the park and offer activities such as nature walks or ice skating. In *Överjärva Gård*, a traditional midsummer festival takes place during the summer solstice. *ekoparken.org*

FOTOGRAFISKA ★ (*14/E4*)

The museum of photography is one of the largest venues of modern photography worldwide. It displays four main exhibitions per year and around 20 small exhibitions. In addition to the large exhibition space, the Fotografiska houses a book and souvenir shop, a restaurant and a photography gallery. **INSIDER TIP** The café on the top floor offers one of the most amazing views over Stockholm. *Sun–Wed 9am–11pm, Thu–Sat 9am–1am | Entrance 145 SEK | Stadsgårdshamnen 22 | fotografiska.eu*

GAMLA STAN ★ (*14/D3*)

The old town is the historic centre of Stockholm and shines with its excellently preserved, mostly 300 to 400-year-old buildings. Impressive merchants' houses line the streets and squares. In the courtyard of the royal castle, the changing of the guard ceremony takes place regularly *(Mon–Sat 12:15, Sun 13:15)*.

INSIDER TIP If you really want to see something, you should strategically position yourself in the courtyard at least 45 minutes before the start of the ceremony in the summer. The *castle (May–Sept daily 10am–5pm | Entrance 160 SEK | www.kungahuset.se)* can be visited. Stortorget, where the Nobel Museum is located, is the heart of the town; it was the former central square.

MODERNA MUSEET (*14/E3*)

Sweden's most famous art museum houses one of the world's largest collections of the French object and conceptual artist, Marcel Duchamp, who passed away in 1968. In front of the building designed by the Spaniard Rafael Moneo is a small park with sculptures by the artist couple Jean Tinguely and Niki de Saint Phalle. Pablo Picasso, Salvador Dali and Louise Bourgeois are among the international artists represented. The view across the water up to Djurgården

The entire Stockholm Old Town is steeped in history

From Skansen Open Air Museum there is a great view of Stockholm

island, from the 🌿 museum café terrace is picture-perfect. The architectural museum is also in the same building, next door to the East Asia museum. *Tue/ Fri 10am–8pm, Wed/Thu/Sat/Sun 10am–6pm | Entrance free | Skeppsholmen | www. modernamuseet.se*

NATIONALMUSEUM *(🛍 14/D2)*
After extensive renovations, Sweden's largest art museum reopened its doors on 13 October 2018. Details on the Internet: *www.nationalmuseum.se*

NOBEL MUSEUM *(🛍 14/D3)*
Here, in the middle of the Old Town, you will find out everything you need to know about Alfred Nobel and the Nobel Prize winners. Underneath each chair in the *Bistro Nobel* you will find

the signature of a Nobel Prize winner. But beware! If you for instance sit on Barack Obama's chair, you are quickly surrounded by scrambling tourists. *June-Aug daily 9am-8pm* clock *| Entrance 120 SEK | Börshuset Stortorget | www. nobelmuseum.se*

SKANSEN ⭐ *(🛍 14/F2)*
The open-air museum on the island of Djurgården exhibits around 150 cultural-historical buildings from all parts of the country. Live animals from the Scandinavian wilderness are in enclosures. The traditional midsummer festival takes place in Skansen in June, and a Christmas market in the winter. The typical Swedish buffet, *smörgåsbord*, is offered in the accompanying restaurant, *Sollidens Matsal*. Take note that here the term smörgås does not mean

sandwiches are served, but a rich buffet with plenty of meat and fish. *May/June 10am–6pm July/Aug 10am-8pm, other months see website | Entrance June-Aug 195, May Sat/Sun 160 SEK, otherwise 125 SEK | Djurgården | www.skansen.se/en*

SÖDERMALM *(⑭ 14/B4)*

The hippest and coolest district of Stockholm, without a doubt. Around Nytorget, Medborgarplatsen and Götgatan you will find the trendiest shops and cafés. And in Söder, as the district is known to the locals, there are also some fantastic viewpoints. Begin your tour at Mariatorget at the Rival Hotel, which belongs to former ABBA musician, Benny Andersson. Continue on *Hornsgatspuckeln (Hornsgatan 24-50)* with its small galleries and original shops (jewellery, tea, clothes) to ⤴ *Monteliusvägen*. There you have a brilliant view over the city and Lake Mälaren. Or do it like the Stockholmers and INSIDER TIP enjoy the view and the (late) sunset in the summer with a picnic on Stockholm's highest mountain, ⤴ *Skinnarviksberget*. If you would rather like to see the Baltic Sea side of Stockholm, go to the ⤴ *Fjällgatan*. During the day, the viewpoint, which allows a nice view of the city, is well visited. From 6pm the panoramic view is all yours – and a few seagulls.

STADSHUSET ⤴ *(⑭ 14/B–C2)*

The brick tower with the three crowns on the top is the landmark of the Swedish capital. The view over Gamla Stan, Södermalm and Kungsholmen is unique. The Nobel Prize Dinner is held in December in the Blue Hall and the Golden Hall of the Town Hall. Apart from the tower, the Stadshuset can only be visited as part of a guided tour. *Tower May-Sept daily 9am–4pm | Entrance 60 SEK | Guided tours in English hourly 10am–3pm | April-Oct 110 SEK, Nov-March 80 SEK | Hantverkargatan 1 | www.stockholm.se/stadshuset*

VASA MUSEUM ★ *(⑭ 14/E2)*

Ship lover or not – you have to come here! As you step into the semi-darkness of the magnificent museum, you face the Vasa: almost 400 years old, 70 metres long and 95% original. The

TRAVEL WITH KIDS

GRÖNA LUND ★

Stockholm's oldest amusement park offers a wealth of fantastic attractions for visitors of all ages. Here the whole family can ride roller coasters at breakneck speed, or scare themselves in Spökhuset. *Greatly varying opening times | Admission from 115 SEK, children under 7 years free, rides extra | Lilla Allmänna Gränd 9 | Djurgården | Tel. 010 7 08 91 00 | www.gronalund. com | www.waxholmsbolaget.se | Bus 67 Liljevalchs/Gröna Lund | S 7 Liljevalchs/Gröna Lund | Ferry from Slussen*

JUNIBACKEN

In the Junibacken children's museum, the little ones are immersed in the world of Astrid Lindgren. Meet Pippi Longstocking at Villa Kunterbunt and visit INSIDER TIP Sweden's largest children's bookstore. With bistro. *June/ August daily 10am–5pm, July daily I 10am-6pm, Sept–May Tue–Sun 10am-5pm | Adults 179 SEK, children up to 15 years 149 SEK | Galärvarvsvägen | Djurgården | Tel. 08 58 72 30 00 | www.junibacken.se*

construction, salvage and significance of the impressive warship, which sank in 1628 on its maiden voyage, is also portrayed in a fascinating and exciting way for those less interested in history. INSIDER TIP Take a look at the introductory film (20 minutes, also in English) and visit the Vasa after 3 pm! Then it is not so crowded anymore. *June–Aug daily 8.30am–6pm | Entrance 130 SEK | Galärvarvsvägen 14 | www.vasamuseet.se*

The Vasa historic warship

CAFÉS & GARDEN CAFÉS

BLÅ PORTEN ★
This quiet, green oasis at Djurgården has a secluded courtyard. Mediter-

ranean cuisine, cakes, sandwiches. *Djurgårdsvägen 64 | Djurgården | www. blaporten.com | Bus 67 | S 7 Liljevalchs/ Gröna Lund*

GRILLSKA HUSET
Fresh, healthy, delicious: in the *Stadsmission* café there are hot dishes, salads, delicious sandwiches and cakes. And: a portion of the revenue goes towards the social work of the Stadtmission. The best place to sit down is the INSIDER TIP quiet courtyard (only in summer, through the café, up the stairs). *Stortorget 3 | Gamla Stan | www.stadsmissionen.se | Bus 2, 53, 57, 55, 76 Slottsbacken | T red, green line Gamla Stan*

INSIDER TIP SATURNUS
The French café has the city's biggest *kanelbullar* (cinnamon buns). They are not cheap, but delicious and worth the price! Patisserie with many delicious calorie bombs. *Also brunch on Sat/Sun. Eriksbergsgatan 6 | Östermalm | www. cafesaturnus.se | Bus 2 Eriksbergsgatan | T red line Östermalmstorg*

SHOPPING

The main shopping streets are close to *Sergels Torg*, just a few minutes' walk from the main train station. The posh fashion boutiques have settled in the *Biblioteksgatan* and the *Birger Jarlsgatan*. The upper-class *Nordiska Kompaniet (NK)* department store in *Hamngatan* is home to many renowned Swedish and international fashion brands and a glass and handicraft department. In *Gamla Stan* there are mainly tourist shops that sell traditional souvenirs such as wooden Dala horses, and small fashion boutiques in *Södermalm* around the *Folkungagatan*.

SHOPPING

Fashion, porcelain, furniture, or accessories: you will find superb designer pieces in Stockholm

Stockholm is a garden of Eden for all design fans! Whether classic or modern – you will find a huge selection of accessories, furniture, fashion and jewellery in the city.

Products designed in Sweden are characterised by simplicity, functionality and clear forms. Many artists and couturiers are still not known abroad yet and this means that you will be able to discover a great deal of fascinating, individual, high-quality design here. For example, mouth-blown glass from the famous Kosta Boda and Orrefors factories, unassuming stoneware crockery in bright colours from Höganäs, linen goods such as tablecloths, place mats and wooden kitchen equipment. The fashion made by local labels including Tiger of Sweden, Acne and Dagmar is exceedingly popular. In trendy *Sofo (South of Folkungagatan www.sofo.se)*, you will find shops that sell offbeat fashion, organic food shops as well as the studios of alternative artists where they sell their handcrafts, jewellery and designs. The CD and record shops between Odenplan and St Eriksplan in Vasastan will seem like paradise to music fans. That is also where many antique shops have become established (Odengatan, Upplandsgata, Roslagsgatan). A visit to the market hall, *Östermalms saluhall*, is an absolute must for any visitor to Stockholm. Wherever you have to wait to be served, it is customary to 'take a number' to show you when it's your turn. Shops usually open Mon–Fri from 10am–6pm and until 2pm or 4pm on Sat. Supermarkets, shopping arcades and Illums, NK and Åhléns department stores stay open longer.

LOW BUDGET

The 50 outlet shops in the Stockholm Quality *Outlet Barkarby* offer 30–70% discounts *(daily | Flyginfarten 4 | Barkaby, Järfälla | www.qualityoutlet. com | suburban train from main station towards Kungsängen or Bålsta: Jakobsberg, then bus 567 to Barkaby Handelsplats)*

MALMÖ

Historical, but at the same time modern and international: that's Malmö, Sweden's third largest city (pop. 323,000).

At the same time, Malmö is the capital and the largest economic centre of the Skåne region *(www.visitskane.com)*. Scania also belonged to Denmark until 1658. The Danish influence and the proximity to the continent are still felt in the city: here everything is a bit livelier and more open than in the rest of Sweden. The climate is milder, the people are more talkative - the reason for a high pub density! About one third of Malmö residents have a migrant background, around 170 countries are represented here! At the *Möllevångstorget* square you'll find shops, and restaurants serving cuisine from around the world. The construction of the Öresund Bridge, which became popular due to the successful TV crime series, *Bron (The Bridge - Transit to Death)* also goes well with this cosmopolitanism. Since 2000 it has connected Malmö with Copenhagen. Together, both cities form a major economic and cultural centre in Northern Europe. Malmö is dominated by green parks, long canals, high-contrast architecture, from the medieval half-timbering to the towering *Turning Torso* in the new, exciting ⊙ eco-district of *Västra Hamnen* - the old working-class city offers colourful diversity and a wide range of art, culture and design for enthusiasts.

And Malmö is strengthening its green initiative. By the year 2020, they want to be the best city in the world in terms of "sustainable urban development". The goal: 100% renewable energy supply by 2030 and 20% reduction in per capita energy consumption. Sustainability is a top priority, for example in the construction of new apartments and districts. Rail transport, bicycle networks and green areas are developed, there is a *Malmö Green Map* for environmentally friendly tourism.

SIGHTSEEING

LILLA TORG (*⋔ 15/B2*)
Cobblestone streets and old half-timbered houses surround this picturesque square with many small shops, pubs and restaurants. In the *Saluhall* (market hall), you can shop and eat very well.

MALMÖ CASTLE (*⋔ 15/A2*)
The Danish King Christian III had the Renaissance castle, Malmöhus built in 1536-52. Today, several museums are housed there: the *Teknikens and Sjöfartens Hus* with vessels from the Viking age to the U-boat from the Second World War. You can follow the history of Malmö and Skåne in the *Stadsmuseet* from the Stone Age to the medieval times. *Daily 10am-5pm | Entrance 40 SEK (applies to all museums) | Malmöhusvägen 6 | www.malmotown.com*

MODERNA MUSEET (*⋔ 15/C2*)
Contemporary and modern art, especially from the 1960s, is presented in an old power station. *Tue–Sun 11am-6pm | Admission 70 SEK | Ola Billgrens place 2–4 | www.modernamuseet.se*

ST. PETER'S CHURCH (*⋔ 15/C2*)
The Gothic brick church from the 14th century is the oldest building in the city of Malmö, with late Gothic paintings, a pulpit from 1599 and a large baroque altar.

The residential and office tower, Turning Torso, strikingly twists itself into the sky

STORTORGET (*🗺 15/B2*)

The old square with the beautiful historic buildings is the centre of *Gamla Staden*, Malmö's Old Town, which is surrounded by moats and canals. The *equestrian statue* portrays Karl X. Gustav, who united Skåne with Sweden in 1658. The Town Hall is also situated here, the former mayor, Jörgen Kock, had it built in the 16th century and it has been redesigned several times.

VÄSTRA HAMNEN ⊛ (*🗺 15/A1*)

The former industrial area and shipyard district in Öresund has developed into a hip district over the past few years, and it is a prime example of sustainable living (energy-efficient houses!) and working. Canals, green areas, a long beach promenade with cafés and restaurants, and beautiful swimming places characterise the image. The 190 m/ 623 ft high modern office and residential complex *Turning Torso* (2005) was designed by the Spanish architect Santiago Calatrava. The 2,000 m²/ 2,400 yd² *Stapelbäddsparken skate park* is also at the Western Harbour.

SHOPPING

The largest shopping area extends from the pedestrian zone to *Stortorget* and *Lilla Torg* via the *Södergatan*, the *Gustav Adolfs Torg*, the *Södra Förstadsgatan* up to the Triangeln and Möllevångstorget squares. *Mobilia*, *Triangeln* and the huge *Emporia* just outside of town *(about 15 minutes by train from Malmö Central Station)* in Hyllie are generously sized shopping meccas.

Design fans should visit the *Designtorget (Södra Förstadsgatan 9)* as well as the *Form Design Centre* in the old half-timbered building, *Hedmanska Gården* (Lilla Torg). Handicrafts can be found at *Formargruppen (Engelbrektsgatan 8)*. On Sundays there is a large *flea market (April–Sept 9am–4pm)* on the Drottningtorget. Both trendy and second-hand goods can be found around the *Davidhallstorg*.

GOTHEN-BURG

The lively cultural metropolis is considered Sweden's gateway to the world. Not only is it an exhibition city, it also houses the largest seaport in Scandinavia.

Even though the city with its 570 000 inhabitants, is only about half the size of Stockholm, Gothenburg is at least just as lively. The Gothenburgers love to sit outside as soon as the temperatures allow it. In the second largest city of the country, you can meet them at the many restaurants with terraces, especially on the boulevards like Kungsportsavenyn or Östra Hamngatan. Gothenburg is an old trading and industrial city, but lately more and more service industries have moved in. Pompous buildings like in Stockholm are few.

FESKEKÖRKA ★ (*16/B2*)

Because the pointed arches of the hall, built in 1874, remind one of a church, the Gothenburgers quickly baptised their fish hall as *Feskekörka* (fish church). Just like the architecture, the freshly caught sea animals which are also offered in the affiliated restaurant, are also worth seeing, (*Moderate*). *Mon-Fri 10am–6pm, Sat 10am–3pm | Rosenlundsvägen | www.feskekörka.se*

GÖTAPLATSEN (*16/D3*)

The square at the southern end of the Kungsportsavenyn was built in 1923 on the occasion of the 300th anniversary of

Gothenburg is nestled on the banks of the Göta älv

SILVIA AND CO.

It is actually surprising that a country in which the concept of equality plays such a large role retains the monarchy. But the fact is: the Swedish royal house is very popular. Scandal- free as far as possible (although there have been some rumours about Carl Gustaf's affairs), the Bernadottes live normal lives and successfully represent Sweden abroad. As head of state, the king does not have political power anymore, but the PR effect of the royal family is enormous.

In addition, Silvia and Co. successfully unite old-fashioned splendour and popularity. They also cleverly mix tradition and modernity and for example lead the female throne succession. The very popular Victoria will therefore inherit from her father one day. Victoria and her siblings, Madeleine and Carl Philip, also delight the people with pictures of glorious family celebrations: weddings, birthdays and baptisms. Carl Gustaf and Silvia now have seven grandchildren.

the city. Around the Poseidon fountain by the Swedish artist Carl Milles, there are an art museum, city theatre, concert hall and a library.

GOTHENBURG HARBOUR AREA ★ (*◻ 16/B1*)

The former industrial district is one of the most interesting areas of the city today. The *paddan*, flat-bottomed excursion boats, take you past the large jetties in the canals *(Departure: Kungsportsplatsen | www.stromma.se/gothenburg)*. On foot, most sights can be seen around the *Packhuskajen*. The opera, which looks like a ship, is situated there, the ⚬⚬ *Utkiken* tower with café and observation deck, as well as the floating maritime museum, *Maritima Centrum*.

GULDHEDEN'S VATTENTORN ⚬⚬

Not far from the Botanical Garden, the Guldheden water tower is tucked away on a hill. Upstairs you have INSIDER TIP a perfect view of the city and surroundings from the café. Inside, the café

exudes an atmosphere between a youth hostel and a grandma's parlour. *Mon–Fri 11am-9pm, Sat 11am-6pm, Sun 11am-8pm | Dr. Sven Johansson's Backe 1 | www.guldhedstornet.se*

KONSTMUSEUM (*◻ 16/D3*)

The focus of the collection is Nordic art, with works from the 15th century to the present. The collection is international, but the thematic focus is on the works of Nordic artists. The Fürstenberg Gallery on the top floor presents paintings by the Nordic painters Ernst Josephson, Carl Larsson and Anders Zorn. *Tue/Thu 11am–6pm, Wed 11am–8pm, Fri–Sun 11am–5pm | Entrance 60 SEK | Götaplatsen/Avenyn | goteborgskonstmuseum.se*

KUNGSPORTSAVENYN ★ (*◻ 16/D3*)

Many shops, restaurants and bars line the magnificent Gothenburg boulevard. In spring the nightlife already pulsates on the many terraces. The Kungsportavenyn and its extension

Östra Hamngatan lead from the harbour to Götaplatsen. The sidewalks are all of 10 meters wide.

LISEBERG
Northern Europe's largest amusement park. In addition to the Ferris wheel and roller coaster, there are also a cinema, shows as well as restaurants and bars. The Balder is considered the most beautiful wooden roller coaster in the world. Those who want something more intense, can try the *Valkyria*, which opened in 2018: you zoom down at 105 km/h/65 mph. *End of April–mid-October, opening hours and entrance fees on the website - there are almost as many ticket options as attractions | Tel. 031 40 01 00 | liseberg.com*

MARITIMA CENTRE (16/B1)
At Packhuskajen, in front of the opera, old mariners, warships, lightships and a submarine have dropped anchor in the maritime centre. *April Sat/Sun 11am–4pm, May/Sept daily 11am–5pm, June–August daily 10am–6pm | Entrance 125 SEK | Packhusplatsen 12 | www.maritiman.se*

RÖDA STEN
An alternative cultural centre on an old factory site, which cultivates a broad concept of art and creates space for unusual and innovative artists. The whole area serves young graffiti artists and those who would like to do it as an experimentation field. Promotion of art starts early here: events are already offered to children from the age of four. Changing programme with art, music and dance. *Tue–Sun noon-5pm, Wed noon–7pm | Entrance 40 SEK | Röda Sten 1 | www.rodasten.com*

SOUTHERN ARCHIPELAGO
The southern archipelago of the city of Gothenburg can be easily reached by tram (last stop: Saltholmen) and ferry. Until the turn of the millennium it was closed to foreigners for military reasons. Today, there are no more such restrictions, and a car-free idyll, with almost 5,000 inhabitants living dispersed on more than a dozen islands, is revealed to the visitor. There are small guesthouses, cafés, restaurants and grocery shops, but most of all, the enjoyment of peace and the sea air.

VÄRLDSKULTURMUSEET
The Ethnological Museum displays objects of different cultures from fashion, art and music. *Tue/Thu/Fri noon–5pm, Wed noon–8pm, Sat/Sun 11am–5pm*

THE FASCINATION WITH THE ELKS

They are the tourists' favourite animal, but the Swedes themselves are sometimes a bit bewildered by the hype that elks trigger in foreign visitors. Many locals like elks in their sights and on the plate. In Sweden, the four major holidays are known as: Christmas, Easter, Midsummer and elk hunting. A good quarter of the 350,000 elk lose their lives during the annual hunting season. Nevertheless – or for that very reason – you do not have to worry about their survival. The elk population in Sweden is healthy. The big problem for elk fanatics, however, is that the animals seldom show up in the wild.

The archipelago is idyllically located directly on the water

*| Entrance free | Södra vägen 54 | www.
varldskulturmuseet.se*

FOOD & DRINK

CAFÉ BROGYLLEN
Cream cake fans will love this pastry shop.
Bread lovers will also get their money's
worth. A lovely view over the Great Canal
from the small ☼ terrace. *Daily | Västra
Hamngatan 2 | www.brogyllen.se*

FOOD TRUCKS
The *Jinx Food Truck (www.jinxfoodtruck.
com) | Budget)* has its place on the Maga-
sinsgatan, in the new hipster area in the
city centre. The owners call their creations
"bastardised Asian food". The queues to
buy the *Thaicos, Porc* and *Vego Buns* are
always long. To prevent isolation, the
Korv United (korvunited.se | Budget) and
the classic herring vendors of *Strömming-
sluckan (www.strommingsluckan.se | Bud-
get)* trucks are right next to it.

SHOPPING & LEISURE

The large shopping centre, 0, is situated
in *Östra Hamngatan*. In the area around
the *Drottninggatan, Korsgatan, Södra Lar-
mgatan, Magasinsgatan* and *Vallgatan*,
there are nice little boutiques as well
as design and furniture stores. In *Design
Torget (Vallgatan 14 | www.designtorget.
se)*, established designers and unknown
artists sell glass, furniture and decorative
items. You can also browse through the
Hague quarter with its antiquarian bookshops, antique collections and second-
hand shops. In the trendy *Linné district*,
right next door, there is a wide range of
second-hand, fashion and art.
The former **INSIDERTIP** *harbour area
(Långgatorna)* is hip and alternative today, with its urban fashion, record and
antique shops. At *Saluhall (Kungstorget
46)*, Gothenburg's old market hall, you
can buy Swedish specialties such as
moose or reindeer.

FOOD & DRINK

The harsh climate and the long-standing importance of agriculture and fishing have left a lasting mark on Sweden's food culture. The traditional dishes are simple, the variety is limited. While the classic Swedish ingredients such as potatoes, fish, meat and mushrooms are of high quality, there are still plenty of tasty dishes in Sweden.

Some Swedish chefs are even among the best at their trade in the world. Over the past few years, they have repeatedly claimed one of the top places in the international cooking world championships. The success is especially reflected in the *Stockholm restaurant scene*. In the capital, there are a handful of establishments that have been awarded at least one Michelin star. The prices are obviously charged accordingly. A cheaper alternative is the daily special, *dagens rätt*, which is offered in many restaurants. It costs around £11/$13 including salad, bread and coffee. By the way, you can refill your coffee as often as you like. This free service is called *Påtår* (= another sip) in Swedish. However, it does not apply to the modern coffee variants such as espresso, latte macchiato or cappuccino.

Gatukök, referred to as *street food*, is part of Swedish culture. The hotdogs and sausages with mashed potatoes served there are certainly not for everyone, but anyone who has not eaten at least once of these takeaways has not experienced the complete Swedish cuisine.

Köttbullar, crayfish and crispbread – the Swedish cuisine satisfies with good products

Asked about their *favourite food*, the standard *answer* of many Swedes is *husmanskost*. These traditional dishes vary from region to region. Herring is often one of them, your smorgasbord wouldn't be complete without pickled herring (sill), and one kind or another of *bullar* – meatballs made of fish *(fiskbullar)* or meat *(köttbullar)*. In addition to bread and butter, you'll often find a type of crispbread *(knäckebröd)* served alongside your main meal. This is what the Swedes tend to reach for.

LOCAL SPECIALITIES

Elk – served as a goulash-like stew (älggryta), or steak (älgbiff)
Fiskbullar – fish cakes that can be bought in the supermarket in cans
Knäckebröd – the classic Swedish dry bread
Köttbullar – meatballs that are mostly eaten with potatoes and sweetened lingon berry jam (lingon)
Tunnbröd – thin bread, a kind of light crispbread from northern Sweden

VISBY/ GOTLAND

Gotland's only ★ town (pop. 23,000) can't hide its medieval roots: the narrow streets and 1 to 12m high houses with stepped gables are surrounded by a more than 3 km/1.8 mi long city wall. The layout of Visby still largely corresponds to 700 years ago, many historic houses have been preserved. *The Gamla Apoteket (Old Pharmacy | Strandgatan)* is especially worth seeing, as it is in an excellent condition. In the former Hanseatic city, there were at least 16 churches during the medieval times, an incredible number for a place of this size. Only the cathedral is still used, the others are ruins or completely destroyed. In the first week of July, the politically interested public from all over Sweden have been meeting in the town since Olof Palmes' time.

SIGHTSEEING

LÄNSMUSEET GOTLAND

The exhibitions of the nine houses and historical sites belonging to *Länsmuseet Gotland (www.gotlandsmuseum.se)* document the artistic and cultural-historical development of the island. The *Art Museum in Visby (Tue–Sun noon–4pm | Admisison 70 SEK | St. Hansgatan 21 | Visby)* mainly displays paintings from the 19th and 20th centuries. In *Fornsalen (Tue–Sun noon–16 pm | Admission 100 SEK | Strandgatan 14 | Visby)*, impressive Viking treasures and medieval church art can be seen.

Petes Museigården (June to Aug daily 11am–5pm | Entrance free | Guided tours 50 SEK | Hablingbo | www.museigardenpetes.se), a faithfully restored 18th century house, is situated in the south. On the terrace with beautiful sea views, coffee and cake is served. There are teas, herbs and juice in the attached shop.

Visby's medieval streets

TRAVEL TIPS

Sweden: the most important information for your trip

BERTHS

▶ STOCKHOLM

Stockholm has two cruise ship docking stations; one near the Old Town, Gamla Stan at Stadsgården quay, another at Freeport (Frihamn), which is about 4 km/2.5 mi from the centre.

▶ VISBY

Visby has a new cruise terminal which opened in 2018.

Other docking stations are in Gothenburg and Malmö.

CLIMATE

A thick sweater belongs in the luggage. At the coasts, the climate is mild with summers that are not too hot, and moderate winters. Inland, summers are hot and winters are cold. But even in Stockholm, the thermometer sometimes drops below minus 10 degrees, and the sun is barely visible. But in summer, daylight lasts much longer: in June it is bright almost around the clock.

CUSTOMS

The EU regulations apply to the import and export of goods to/from Sweden. The following quantities are used as guide values for imports and exports: 10 l of spirits, 20 l of dessert wines, 90 l of wine or 110 l of beer. In addition, there are the general maximum limits of 800 cigarettes or 200 cigars (www.tullverket.se). U.S. citizens may enter Sweden without a visa for up to 90 days for tourist or business purposes.

INTERNET & WIFI

Many cafés, restaurants and hotels, and also most towns and cities in Sweden offer their guests free WiFi. On trains and buses, the free internet is also often a standard service.

MONEY & CREDIT CARDS

Although Sweden is a member of the European Union, the national currency remains the Swedish krona (SEK). But you do not need to worry about exchanging money. Cash is out, and you can really pay for everything by credit card (with Maestro or V-Pay feature). If you still want bills and coins, it's best to obtain it from ATMs or exchange it at a foreign exchange. Hardly any bank in Sweden still offers an exchange service.

BUDGETING

Coffee	£2.5/$3
	for a cup of coffee
Beer	about £4.5/$5.5
	for 0.4 litres
Ice cream	£3.6/$4.4
	for three scoops on a waffle

DENMARK

It is said that the Danes are the happiest (or second happiest) people in the world: fond of children, private, yet friendly and open.

The keyword is "Hyggelig" – a term describing happiness and coziness. Why is it that people are happy here? Perhaps also because of the beauty of their country: on the west coast alone, over 400 km/250 mi of beaches and dunes extend from the holiday island, Rømø in the Wadden Sea, high up to Grenen's northern point, at the former artists' colony, Skagen, of which the Nordic lights are still famous. The major cultural and shopping centres are also close to the sea: Aarhus at Kattegat and Aalborg at the Limfjord, the country's biggest fjord. The Danish forests are a kind of secret tip and still offer real destinations for explorers and nature fans. About 14 percent of the country is made up of forests. The capital island, Zealand, has a very rich history. Nowhere else in the country are there as many castles and manors as here and on the neighbouring Funen. And next to the capital, Copenhagen, is Roskilde and Zealand's former royal seat. Which brings us to a piece of tradition that is as dear to the thoroughly democratic Danes as it is expensive: the royal house. Denmark is loyal to the king or queen and firmly supports the artistically talented regent, Margrethe II. The world-famous LEGO® brick was invented by the Dane Ole Kirk Christiansen in the town of Billund in 1949.

Balanced people, internationally acclaimed design and fantastic landscapes: Denmark is a real gem in many ways

RØNNE/ BORNHOLM

Administrative seat and thus "capital" of the island, Bornholm, largest ferry harbour, most populace place – and yet only a small town with just over 13,500 inhabitants.

A market town, picturesque, friendly and well-structured in an old centre. 3 km/1.9 mi From north to south, 2 km/1.2 mi from west to east. Half-timbered houses still dominate the cityscape, vertical and horizontal beams without inclinations, give the architecture peace and harmony. Half-timber also holds the white church above the harbour together, which is a second landmark (after the lighthouse) for the sailors – and the expectant holidaymakers on the ferries. It was originally built at the end of the 13th century and is named differently, as it should be on an island, after the saint of the sailors, Nicholas.

SIGHTSEEING

BORNHOLM'S FORSVARSMUSEUM ☼ (*① 16/–C4*)

Anyone interested in military history will find weapons, uniforms and models of fortresses in the Defence Museum. The collections tell of the defence of the island in earlier times until the end of the Second World War. The fort tower, built in 1688 on the *Galløkken*, the old gallows hill, is a few steps south. It remained from a citadel that was never completed. *Arsenalvej 8 | May–Sept Mon–Fri 10am–4pm | 55 DKK | bornholmsforsvarsmuseum.dk*

BORNHOLM'S MUSEUM (*① 17/C2*)

The collections display findings from the early history, geological, zoological and ethnological exhibits. With its corner shop, doctor's practice and living rooms, it gives insight into the "good old days". The most valuable exhibits of the museum are probably the guldgubber, 2,300 small figures in wafer-thin gold leaf shaped pieces, which were found in 1985 near Svaneke. They are from the 6th and 7th centuries, and probably represent offerings. *Sankt Mortensgade 29 | Mid May–June and mid Aug–mid Oct Mon–Sat, July–mid Aug daily 10am–5pm | 70 DKK | www.bornholmsmuseum.dk*

ERICHSEN'S GÅRD ★ (*① 17/B2*)

Erichsen's farm (gård means yard, not garden) is a dependence of the Bornholm Museum. The spacious but not showy commoner's house in the old quarter between the market and harbour, built in 1806 as a tobacco factory and expanded in 1840, was the residence of chancellor Thomas Erichsen and

Colourful half-timbered houses and cobblestone streets in the old town of Rønne

ROUND CHURCHES

The four bumpy churches from the 12th or 13th Century, which look so different from most other sacred and secular buildings on the island, have become the landmarks of Bornholm. The *Østerlars Kirke* in the east, 5 km/3 mi from Gudhjem, is the largest. In the almost equally large *Ols Kirke* high up in the north, between Tejn on the east and Vang on the west coast, has a beautiful Renaissance pulpit and the impressive Romanesque font attracts art lovers. The *Ny Kirke* near Rønne is the smallest round church; many visitors consider it the most beautiful church. The *Nylars Kirke*, just a few kilometres from Rønne on the road to Aakirkeby, is believed to have the best acoustics of the four round churches. The experts have long assumed that all four round churches were old fortified churches during the middle ages: fortress, camp and church, all in one. The conical roofs, which characterises this unusual type of church, and also a part of the Bornholm landscape, were first erected centuries after the construction of the churches. *rundkirker.dk*

his family for more than 100 years. The legends around the artists and positive people associated with this house and its former inhabitants, are very delicate. Holger Drachmann (1846–1908), the painter poet from the world-famous Skagen colony and Erichsen's daughter, Vilhelmine, who was called Belli, are remembered with special rooms. Vilhelmine married Kristian Zahrtmann (1843–1917) – he also painted the beautiful Vilhelmine; and Elisabeth Zahrtmann, his sister, in turn married an Erichsen son. *Laksegade 7 | Mid–May–mid Oct. Fri/Sat 10am–4pm | 50 DKK | www.bornholmsmuseum.dk*

HJORTH´S FACTORY (*17/B2*)
Hjorth's Factory is also a dependence of the Bornholm Museum: a successful mix of functioning workshop, museum, gallery and salesroom. The house dates back to 1859 and provides a good overview of the history of industrial and artistic ceramics production in Bornholm. *Krystalgade 5 | Mid–May–Mid-Oct Mon–Sat 10am–5pm, March–mid–May | 70 DKK | www.bornholmsmuseum.dk*

OLD TOWN ★ (*17/B2*)
The starting point and meeting place is the lively market square *(Store Torv)* and the distinct sculpture created by June-Ichi Inoue in 2000, is the best of all. The Japanese artist lived in the north of the island until his death in 2009. The sculpture is intended to symbolise the history and constant spiritual development of man. It is also a perfect annual clock: on 24 June, during midsummer, the sun shines precisely through the slit of the sophisticated sculpture.

Stroll down the *Snellemark* street, down towards the harbour and then left into *Storegade*, towards *Kirkepladsen*. *Kirkestræde*, *Larsegade* and *Vimmelskaftet* can mark the next route. The smallest house in the city is in *Vimmelskaftet 11*. Almond, apricot and fig trees thrive next to the building in *Sankt Hans Stræde 3*. From the Rendegade the path goes through quiet streets – *Lille Mortens-*

gade, Slippen and Bagergade – to Søndergade. Here, at house no. 14, is the former merchant house and warehouse of a ship owner from 1813, with a lookout from the attic. Then you come to the *Hovedvagt* (main police station), built in 1744 from stones of the Hammershus ruins, and past the old theatre back to the market.

A second stroll leads to the north of the old town: in the *Laksegade* stands *Erichsens Gaard* (see separate entry), in *Rosengade* on the corner of Storegade is *Kommandantgården*, where mulberry trees grow in the courtyard. *Storegade* Street was once the street of the upper class. No. 36, the *Amtmandsgården*, still bears witness to this prosperity. In *Grønnegade*, *Fiskerstræde*, *Krystalgade* and Havnegade, photographers, painters and history-conscious explorers will find all sorts of scenic nooks.

ST. NICOLAI KIRKE ☆ (*[1] 17/B3*)

The town church of Rønne is dedicated to the patron saint of sailors, St. Nicholas. The original structure is from the 13th and 14th century. The present-day look was created after 1915; as it was completely rebuilt and renovated inside, the experts speak of a new building. The following are vintage pieces: the Gothic baptismal font, the gallery (1721) and two of the three bells. Concerts that take place in this place of worship during the summer festival season are in high demand because of the good acoustics and the intimate atmosphere.

FOOD & DRINK

DI 5 STÄUERNA

Rønne's gourmet restaurant in the Fredensborg Hotel at the southern end of the city. Quality, ideas, service, prices: everything of the highest standard and

has been for many years. *Strandvejen 116 | Tel. 56 90 44 44 | closed for lunch | Expensive*

GREEN SOLUTION HOUSE RESTAURANT ✪

Sustainable cuisine under the management of chef Kasper Beyer. Classic dishes made exclusively from local and organic ingredients are served. The attached hotel also treats the environment in a responsible manner. The restaurant is very popular, so make a reservation. *Strandvejen 79 |Tel. 56 95 1913 | closed on Sun | www.greensolutionhouse.dk | Moderate–Expensive*

SHOPPING

BENT SVENDBORG PETERSEN

Since 1994, Bent has continued the tradition of his father, Aage, who after the Second World War had begun to make replicas of famous Bornholm longcase clocks all over the world. Be sure to take a look at his workshop, marvel at the incredible number of small screws and cogwheels, which are put together into a masterpiece after weeks of tedious work. Until about 1900, when American clocks superseded the good old Bornholm clocks, there were over 50 watchmakers alone in Rønne; it supplied around 330 clocks a year to Copenhagen and another 150 to the rest of Denmark and abroad. Today, Bent and his four employees build and sell at least 30 to 40 clocks per year. *Torneværksvej 26 (between swimming pool and bowling alley)*

IM GENBRUG

Used, and for a good cause! In this Diaconal Inner Mission store, you can find clothes and household goods at bargain prices. *Haslevej 2*

INSIDER TIP OSTE-HJØRNET

For over 20 years, Birgit Gren Hansen has satisfied the appetites of Bornholm locals for delicatessen. Here you will find the best cheeses of the whole island. In addition, at Oste-Hjørnet (in English: "The cheese corner") one can buy fresh bread, tasty cold meat and other specialties produced in Bornholm. *Østergade 40 b*

WHERE TO GO

ARNAGER

The small harbour in front of the old fishing and farming village, 6 km/ 3.8 mi south of Rønne, is a small sight: because of the silting risk, it was built far out in the sea, 200m from the cliff, in 1884. A wooden bridge connects the pier with the place. Bank swallows and other rare birds nest here; various rock layers alternate between Sosebucht and Madsegrav *(Fosforitten)* on the Arnagerstrand, a picture book of geological history. The *passage tomb (jættestue)* is a popular destination. It was only discovered in the middle of the 20th century; 25 people had found their last rest here in the Neolithic period (around 2500 BC). A signpost at the entrance marks the way towards it.

NY KIRKE ★

The smallest round church of the island, 6 km/3.8 mi northeast of Rønne in the village of *Nyker*, also its most beautiful church. The beautifully painted frieze on the thick centre column deserves special attention. The exact year of construction is unknown, but is probably, like the other round churches, from before 1150. The pulpit was carved in 1610. The bell tower stands alone, as usual. Right next to the church, in an old blacksmith's shop (1860), the textile artist *Bente Hammer (Nyker Hovedgade 32)* has her workshop and sales room.

The Ny Kirke is one of Bornholm's typical round churches

FOOD & DRINK

Danish chefs have set a trend with New Nordic cuisine

Junior and young Danish chefs such as René Redzepi, Kenneth Hansen and Allan Poulsen, Nikolaj Kirk, Morten Nielsen or the twins Jesper and Richard Koch, have swapped the former national dish of potatoes with plenty of brown sauce for international creations with flair.

But it is especially thanks to Claus Meyer that Denmark is no longer a *terra incognita* on the gastronomy map: a few years ago, the Copenhagen star chef, together with other top Scandinavian chefs, launched the initiative of a "New Nordic Cuisine" and committed himself to a *new Danish dining experience*. The basis for this is the "Nordic Kitchen Manifesto". His main objective: "Only selected, fresh raw materials from the relevant region are used for our dishes," says Claus Meyer. Even the professionals have long recognised Denmark's gastronomic quality: *many awards* by internationally recognised gastronomic critics are the result. It goes without saying that this goodness has its price. However, many rural restaurants in Denmark, and *Kros*, the country inns, are still tradition-conscious; here you will find typical dishes, mostly with fish and meat, as in the past and at prices of £28/$34–£37/$45 for the main course. More important than a restaurant, however, is the *local baker*; sweetness has its firm, firmly entrenched place in Danish life. The number of puff pastry creations is legendary; the creams with which the pastry is filled are famous. The poppy seed rolls are called *birkes*, and are feather-light, and only the poppy seeds sprinkled on them gives them any weight at all. *Rundstykker* (rolls) are actually so round, as promised by their name: they are the backbone of the bun craft. Buns and breads with seeds are being offered more and more frequently, even rye bread *(rugbrød)* is fortified. Every baker who keeps his eye on things has his own blends in the programme: not just baked goods, but also small, nutritious treats. Something has been set in motion in Denmark.

COPENHAGEN

The capital of Denmark (pop. 1.2 million) actually consists of two completely independent parts.

In the Old Town, nightlife, culture and business thrive; it's all about big and small politics. Outside this narrow and easily manageable area, the city loses itself in confusion: suburbs, motorway junctions and uncontrolled growth. Because Copenhagen is still growing – at an increasing rate. Since the opening of the bridge over the Øresund in 2000, a new era has begun for the Øresund region.

SIGHTSEEING

AMAGERTORV (🕮 18/C2)

At Amagertorv the *Illums Bolighus* lures with Danish design, the *Royal Copenhagen* sells porcelain, glass and silver in a beautiful Renaissance building. In summer, when tables and chairs are in front of the *Café Norden* and the *Café Europa* and the young Copenhageners crowd the Stork fountain (1894), it's a matter of seeing and being seen. The most beautiful house is certainly No. 6, which was built in the Dutch Renaissance style in 1616. On the Amagertorv you should not miss a typical Danish hotdog at one of the sausage stalls *(pølsevogn)*.

DANSK JØDISK MUSEUM (DANISH-JEWISH MUSEUM) ★ (🕮 18/C–D3)

In October 1943, the Copenhagen residents rescued about 7,200 Jews from deportation to German concentration camps. The Jews managed to escape via Øresund to Sweden, where it was safe. The history of this rescue operation, the culture and art of the Jews living in Denmark, are portrayed by the Danish Jewish Museum. The interior design and exhibition concept in Galejhus, a former boathouse on Slotsholmen, was created by Daniel Libeskind, who also designed the Jewish Museum in Berlin. Libeskind leads visitors through a labyrinth of slanted walls and fractured passageways, past 3,000 exhibits that were privately owned or made available by the Jewish communities of Denmark. *Sept–May Tue–Fri 1pm–4pm, Sat/Sun noon–5pm, June–Aug Tue–Sun 10am–5pm | Admission 60 DKK | Christians Brygge/Proviantpassagen | www.jewmus.dk | Bus 1A, 2A, 66 Det Kongelige Bibliotek*

DEN LILLE HAVFRUE (LITTLE MERMAID) ★

What a scandal! Under the protection of the night vandals sawed off the head of the Little Mermaid in 1964. There she sat on her boulder at Langlinie without head and curls. In 1998, her head and arm were separated a second time; In 2003, strangers pushed the maiden into the water. But whatever was inflicted

Copenhagen's central square: the Amagertorv

The Copenhagen Town Hall dominates the square named after it

on the Little Mermaid, the scars have healed, and the Little Mermaid is looking in love again, dreamy and a little sad about the Øresund – as she was created by Edvard Eriksen. The sculptor had received the order and the money from the brewer Carl Jacobsen. He was so moved by Hans Christian Andersen's love story of the little mermaid and her prince that he wanted to give the city a landmark. *Langelinie | Bus 26 Indiakai, Søndre Frihavn*

DESIGN MUSEUM DANMARK (🏛 18/E1)

Denmark's great designers are presented with their classics in the world's largest collection of Danish design objects: Børge Mogensen chairs, Poul Kjærholm chairs and lamps by Poul Henningsen. *April–Oct Tue, Thu–Sun 10am–6pm, Wed 10am–9pm | Admission 1 DKK | Bredgade 68 | www.designmuseum.dk | Bus 1A, 15 esplanades | Metro Kongens Nytorv*

NATIONAL MUSEET (NATIONAL MUSEUM) (🏛 18/C3)

The sun chariot is the star of the National Museum. The gilded sun disc, drawn by a horse, dates back to 1400 BC. Then you are spoilt for choice: objects from prehistory and early history, finds from the Viking Age, the Renaissance or from Denmark's recent history (1660 to today) with a section on daily life among nobles, commoners, artisans and peasants, which is shown by costumes, furniture and silver. In addition, there is the royal *coin cabinet* with coins from antiquity to the Vikings, to modern times and Danish gold medals from 1550 to 2000 and the ethnological department, which equals a world tour. *Tue–Sun 10am–5pm | Admission 75 DKK | Ny Vestergade 10 | www.natmus.dk | Bus 1A, 2A, 14, 15, 26, 40 Stormbroen*

RÅDHUS (TOWN HALL) (🏛 18/B3)

The small polar bears on the ridge of the Town Hall are a Nordic accessory to the Italian Renaissance style, by which the architect Martin Nyrop was inspired in Siena, Italy. Next to the main entrance Jens Olsen's impressive, *Verdensur* (World Clock) ticks with twelve drives that track the courses of the sun and stars as well as the Gregorian and Julian calendars next to the times around the world. From the 106 m/ 350 ft high Town Hall tower with its 300 steps, you have a fantastic view over the city. *Viewing Mon–Fri 9am–5pm, Sat 9:30am–1pm, guided tour Mon–Fri 1pm, Sat 10am, tower tours Mon–Fri 11am and 2pm, Sat noon, World Clock Mon–Fri 9am–5pm, Sat 10am–1pm | Town Hall tour 50 DKK, visit the tower 30 DKK | www.kk.dk | Bus 2A, 5A, 6A, 26, 29, 250S Rådhuspladsen*

STRØGET ★ (*⑭ 18/B–D, 2–3*)

On city maps you will usually search for the Strøget ("shopping") in vain – you do not need to either. You can't miss the Strøget. Suddenly you are in the middle of the shopping route, which meanders from Rådhuspladsen for a good 2 km/1.2 mi to Kongens Nytorv. The Town Hall square stands for the new, democratic Copenhagen, the Kongens Nytorv for the old, royal Copenhagen. Near the Town Hall there are still fast- food chains, soft serve, souvenir shops and exchange offices, but with every metre further in the direction of Kongens Nytorv, the displays in the shop windows become more exclusive and expensive. The end of Strøget, the Østergade, has always been Copenhagen's finest address. At the end of the 18th century the sidewalks were already covered with tiles, so that the ladies could stroll with clean feet. In 1962 Strøget was declared the first pedestrian zone in Europe. It has remained the longest to date.

OPERAEN ★ (*⑭ 18/E2*)

Who should pay for it? For a long time this question concerns the people and the parliament. Ship owner and container billionaire Mærsk McKinney Møller was finally fed up with this debate. Without hesitation, he paid his compatriots 335 million kroner for the construction of the opera house. The architect Henning Larsen was commissioned to build a world-class opera, with outstanding acoustics – a tricky task. The flat roof that towers over the opera at a height of 24 m/80 ft and protrudes 32 m/105 ft over the entrance is certainly a noteworthy feature. If you look closely, you will see how the opera reflects the city in the massive glass arch. *Guided tours 120 DKK, also in English, are offered several times a day. Holmen | www.operaen.dk | Harbour bus 901, 902*

RUNDETÅRN (ROUND TOWER) ☼ (*⑭ 18/C2*)

A 34 m/112 ft high tower without stairs – how to get to the top? Christian IV did not know the comfort of an elevator

LOW BUDGET

Admission is free in some museums on certain days of the week, for example, in the *Ny Carlsberg Glyptotek* on Tuesday and on Wednesday in the *Nikolaj Kunsthal* and in the *Thorvaldsens Museum*.

☼ Aiming high for a few crowns: experience Copenhagen from above in the restaurant of the department store *Illum*, from the *Rundetårn* in the city, from the *Marmorkirken* dome, from the *Town Hall Tower* or from the top of the tower of *Vor Frelsers Kirke*.

today. He wanted to get onto the top platform with his horse and cart and had a 206-meter-long continuous stairless spiral passage constructed. Until 1861, the tower served as the observatory of the University of Copenhagen. Freed from old plaster, today you can see how the bricks were laid in alternating red and yellow courses. From the observation deck of the Round Tower you have a wonderful view of the Old Town of Copenhagen. *May–Sept daily 10am–8pm | Admission 25 DKK | Købmagergade | www.rundetaarn.dk | Metro, Bus 5A, 6A, 14 Nørreport*

AMALIENBORG SLOT (AMALIENBORG PALACE) ★ (*⌘ 18/D-E2*)

The queen lives here, more precisely, in the south-eastern of the four palaces. When she's home, the Danish flag, the Dannebrog, is flying on the roof. It was the idea of Frederik V. (1723–66) to build four palaces around the octagonal Amalienborg castle square. Since the king did not want to build himself, he gave the building plots to the Privy Councillor, Joachim von Brockdorff, the Earl of Levetzau, the Baron Severin Løvenskjold and the Count Adam Moltke. But that's not all, the wealthy builders were taxed for 40 years. In 1750, construction began on the designs of court architect Nicolai Eigtved. No one suspected that 50 years later, the royal family would move into the Rococo palace. When Christiansborg Castle burnt down in 1794 and Christian VI. became homeless, the royal family bought the four palaces. Since then, Amalienborg has been the residence of the Danish kings. You can visit the ground floor of the Levetzau Palace, where Christian VIII once resided. *May–October–daily 10am–4pm | Admission 95 DKK | dkks.dk/amalienborg-palace | Bus 1A, 15, 19 Bredgade*

ROSENBORG CASTLE ★ (*⌘ 18/C1*)

In the royal summer palace of Christian IV, you can see everything you al-

The Little Mermaid, Copenhagen's most famous landmark

SHOPPING

Whether made by hand or manufactured industrially: Danish design is world famous

Danish design is of classical beauty and is known worldwide as synonymous with Scandinavian elegance. The variety is great, whether glass from Holmegaard or the local glass artist, porcelain from Royal Copenhagen or the ceramicist at the resort. The fashion designers from the little kingdom with labels like Saks Potts and Ganni are becoming more and more famous. You can go shopping in Copenhagen, Aarhus, Aalborg and Odense.

CANDLES

Candles in Danish are called levende lys: living light – a clear indication of its significance in Denmark. They are usually not expensive because they are produced in large numbers and industrially. However, in many places and in the rural districts, you will also find artisans offering handmade candles. You can easily buy them online, but you'll have a nicer memory of it, if they are bought at a shop.

FURNITURE & LIVING

Furniture design from Denmark follows the classically beautiful furnishing trend. Danish designers stand for clean lines, functionality and timelessness. Designer pieces or architectural furniture, classics from Arne Jacobsen's armchair "The Swan" to chairs by Hans J. Wegner, or handy kitchen helpers from Stelton or Rosti Mepal can for example be found at Kollund Møbler *(www.kollund.dk)* in Kollund, just behind the Flensburg border. Tønder on the west coast is also a popular shopping spot. Companies such as Bolia *(www.bolia.com)* and BoConcept *(www.boconcept.com)* also run furniture and home accessories shops in the UK. For more than 40 years, Nyt ibo *(Store Kongensgade 88 | www.nytibo.dk)*, in the heart of Copenhagen, has been best in Scandinavian furniture design, be it furniture, lamps or carpets, and whether for living or dining room, bedroom, office, garden or terrace.

ways wanted to know about the royal family: clothes, jewellery, porcelain, toys, portraits, even the corridor to the toilet is documented. *Entrance Øster Voldgade 4a | April–mid–June daily 10am–3pm, mid–June–mid Sept 9am–5pm | Admission 110 DKK | www.kongernessamling.dk*

TIVOLI ★ (*18/B3*)

Funfair – that would be an insult. Well, there are carrousels, a dizzying roller coaster, game booths, ticket sellers. There are coffees and cakes, more than 40 restaurants, theatre performances danced or dreamed in tranquil green alcoves with water features. But here is no screaming, no booming music. It is a park to please all the senses. "If the people are amused, it does not politicise." With these words, the journalist Georg Carstensen (1812–57) convinced King Christian VIII to build an amusement park in front of the city walls. The king said yes, and on August 15, 1843, Tivoli opened. *Admission 110 DKK (rides cost extra!) | Vesterbrogade 3 | Information and opening hours: www.tivoli.dk | S-tog København H (Hovedbanegård) | Bus 1A, 2A, 5A, 6A, 26, 29, 40 Rådhus*

CAFÉS

CAFÉ MANDELA ⊙

Compared to the other hip spots around the Halmtorvet, there is a pleasantly relaxed atmosphere here. Small dishes with organic ingredients, children under 12 pay half. Fri and Sat from 10pm live music. *Daily. | Onkel Dannys Plads 9 | Bus 10 Gasværksvej*

INSIDER TIP ▶ OVEN VANDE

Whether in wicker chairs outside or at the white-covered bistro table – here, the whole Christianshavn meets for a sandwich or fish dish. The prices are pleasing. *Daily | Overgaden Oven Vandet 44 | Metro Christianshavn*

INSIDER TIP ▶ PROPS COFFEE SHOP

Typical of Nørrebro: there is a mix of everything in the smallest of spaces – generations, religions, languages and skin colours. Everything that you eat and drink at is second-hand. *Daily | Blågårdsgade 5 | Bus 3A, 5A Elmegade*

SHOPPING

In the car-free shopping street *Strøget* you will mostly find familiar products:

CHILD IN THE BOX

The three-wheeled transport bikes are part of the cityscape. They were invented by the inhabitants of Christiania. The dropouts needed a vehicle with which they could transport their belongings in their Free State. Of course, anything that runs on petrol was out of the question. The solution: the bike with the box in front of the steering wheel. Such a bike is not cheap: the basic, no-frills box bike costs about £1400/$1680. Practically everything can be transported through the city in it. However, it is mostly the heads of little Copenhageners that peep out of the boxes. And when it rains, a cover is simply put over it.

Beautiful on the outside and exciting from inside: Rosenborg Castle

fashion houses with mass-produced goods and boutiques with international designer fashion.

What remains are the fine Danish addresses in terms of silver, crystal and porcelain at the *Amagertorv* . You will find stylish souvenirs in the design department store *Illums Bolighus*. In the city centre – Danish Indre By – you should leave Strøget and immerse yourself in the side streets. The international and expensive fashion designers are hiding in the quarter between Købmagergade , Kronprinsensgade and Antonigade.

Copenhagen's antique scene has a great reputation. The dealers, whose shops are like museums, have settled around the Amalienborg Palace in *Bredgade*; more can be found in the *Kompagnistræde* and *Læderstræde*. The shops and boutiques in *Vesterbro* are younger and crazier. Designers and artists with their own studios have settled down along *Istedgade* and *Vesterbrogade*. You may find the shops in the multi-cultural *Nørrebro* too freaky. Nevertheless, a stroll around the *Sankt Hans Torv* and through the *Elmegade* is worth it – even if you just marvel.

You love it more middle-class, dignified? Then you will feel comfortable in *Østerbro* . The streets in this part are lined with well-kept facades and a lot of greenery, suggesting that the crowns are spent easier here. The boutiques, shoe stores and delicatessens in the *Østerbrogade, Willemoesgade* and *Classensgade* are just as upper-class. Regardless of the quarter you stroll through in Copenhagen, you have a good chance of finding something that you don't have at home.

SKAGEN

Skagen – that sounds like the sea, rough, wild nature, fish and art.

Artists such as Michael Ancher and Peder Severin Krøyer from Copenhagen discovered the fascination of the fishing village (pop. 8,200) at the turn of the 20th century. It was the very special light that inspired them. Skagen was first an artist colony, then seaside resort. But beware: the currents at *Grenen*, the outer headland of Skagen, are treacherous – swimming here is therefore prohibited.

Brøndums Hotel is a heritage house, still full of style and attitude. This is where the painter Michael Ancher stayed when he came to Skagen. Later he married the daughter of the house, Anna Brøndum. She too became a famous painter. Their *house (Markvej 2–4 | May–Sept daily, otherwise Tue–Sun 10am–5pm | Admission 80 DKK* is an artist's idyll. The world of Skagen painters is brought to life in *Skagen's Museum (info & opening times at: www.skagensmuseum.dk)*, which features many of Krøyer's and Anchers' major works.

The *Skagen Odde Nature Centre (info & opening times: www.skagen-natur.dk)* is an experience. At 1,500m², the adventure museum illustrates how wind, water, light and sand have changed the northern tip of Denmark for thousands of years – almost everything can be playfully tested with experiments. *Bodilles Kro (Østre Strandvej 11 | Tel. 98 44 33 00 | www.bodilleskro.dk | moderate)* is always a good address for fish lovers: the clams are excellent.

This is the Danish joy of living and Danish pure summer: at the *Solnedgangkiosken* (sunset kiosk) 500 meters west of the village in Gammel Skagen you can enjoy a cold beer, meet nice people, small talk with them, and experience the unforgettable sunset experience together.

10 km/6 mi south of Skagen, Denmark's largest wandering dune moves inexorably to the east, Råbjerg Mile: up to 15 m/50 ft high, the protected natural wonder will reach the Baltic Sea in about 200 years. *www.skagen-tourist.dk.*

House for peace seekers: on a dune in Skagen

TRAVEL TIPS

Denmark: the most important information for your trip

BANKS, PRICES & MONEY

Opening hours for banks and savings banks are usually *Mon–Fri 10am–4pm, Thu 10m–6pm*. The price range in Denmark is slightly higher than in the UK. Spirits are about 10 percent more expensive. Food costs about 20 percent more than in the UK. The official means of payment is the Danish krone, the euro is accepted at most areas near the border. Major credit cards are generally accepted, but fees are often charged.

BERTHS

▶ COPENHAGEN

Copenhagen has several cruise ship docking stations; from the newest quay, where the majority of ships moor, the city centre is approximately 7 km/ 4.5 mi away.

▶ SKAGEN

Skagen harbour is located near the town centre.

There is another docking station in Rønne at Bornholm.

HEALTH

In hospitals, tourists are entitled to free treatment. Any necessary return transport to your home country is at your own expense. Otherwise, your statutory health insurance entitles you to free medical treatment and reimbursement of doctor, dentist and medication costs. The European Health Insurance Card from your health insurance must be presented when you seek medical treatment or purchase medicines.

OPENING HOURS

The Danish shop-closing law leaves it to the owner when he wants to open, therefore the times *(usually Mon–Fri 9/10–5:30pm/6pm, Thu or Fri to 7pm/8pm, Sat till noon/4pm or 8pm)* vary. On the 1st and last Sunday of the month shops open from *10m-5pm*. The opening times of the restaurants and inns vary widely.

WEATHER

In summer, the sun shines on Denmark as often as on Bavaria. At the west coast, the constant wind causes the sun to feel less harsh and so deceives the true strength of the rays. So do not forget a strong sunscreen.

BUDGETING

Snack	£2.7/$3.3	*for a Pølser*
Beer	£5/$6	*for a small one*
Coffee	£3.2/$3.9	*for a cup*

USEFUL PHRASES

	ENGLISH	GERMAN	POLISH
IN BRIEF	yes/no/maybe	ja/nein/vielleicht	tak/nie/może
	please/thank you	bitte/danke	Proszę./Dziękuję.
	Sorry!	Entschuldige!	Przepraszam!
	Excuse me!	Entschuldigen Sie!	Przepraszam pana/panią!
	May I ...?	Darf ich ...?	Czy mogę ...?
	Pardon?	Wie bitte?	Słucham?
	I would like to ...	Ich möchte ...	Chciałbym ...
	Have you got ...?	Haben Sie ...?	Czy ma pan/pani ...?
	How much is ...?	Wie viel kostet ...?	Ile kosztuje ...?
	I (don't) like this.	Das gefällt mir (nicht).	To mi się (nie) podoba.
	good/bad	gut/schlecht	dobrze/źle
	open/closed	offen/geschlossen	otwarte/zamknięte
SALUTATION & TRAVEL	Good morning!/ afternoon!	Guten Morgen!/ Tag!	Dzień dobry!
	Good evening!/ night!	Guten Abend! Gute Nacht	Dobry wieczór!/ Dobranoc!
	Hello!/Goodbye!	Hallo!/Auf Wiedersehen	Witam!/Do widzenia!
	Bye!	Tschüss!	Cześć!
	My name is ...	Ich heiße ...	Nazywam się ...
	What's your name?	Wie heißen Sie?	Jak pan/pani się nazywa?
	I'm from ...	Ich komme aus ...	Pochodzę z ...
	station/harbour	Bahnhof/Hafen	dworzec/port
	departure/arrival	Abfahrt/Ankunft	odjazd/przyjazd
	What time is it?	Wie viel Uhr ist es?	Która godzina?
	It's three o'clock.	Es ist drei Uhr.	Jest godzina trzecia.
	today/tomorrow/ yesterday	heute/morgen/ gestern	dziś/jutro/ wczoraj
FOOD & DRINK	The menue, please.	Die Speisekarte, bitte.	Czy mogę prosić kartę?
	May I have ...?	Könnte ich bitte ... haben?	Chciałbym/chciałabym ...?
	knife/fork/spoon	Messer/Gabel/Löffel	nóż/widelec/łyżka
	salt/pepper/sugar	Salz/Pfeffer/Zucker	sól/pieprz/cukier
	vinegar/oil	Essig/Öl	ocet/olej
	milk/cream	Milch/Sahne	mleko/śmietana
	with/without ice	mit/ohne Eis	z lodem/bez lodu
	vegetarian	Vegetarier(in)	wegetarianin/wegetarianka
	May I have the bill, please?	Ich möchte zahlen, bitte.	Proszę o rachunek!

Short and sweet

This short list of phrases will help you say the most important words and phrases in the languages listed below:

LITHUANIAN	LATVIAN	ESTONIAN
taip/ne/galbūt	jā/nē/varbūt	jah/ei/võib olla
prašau/ačiū	lūdzu/paldies	Palun./Tänan.
Atsiprašau!	Atvaino!	Vabandust!
Atsiprašau!	Atvainojiet!	Vabandage!
Ar galėčiau ...?	Vai drīkstu ...?	Kas ma tohin ...?
Kas?	Kā, lūdzu?	Kuidas palun?
Aš noriu ...?	Es vēlos ...	Ma tahan ...?
Ar turite ...?	Vai jums ir ...?	Kas teil on ...?
Kiek kainuoja ...?	Cik maksā ...?	Kui palju see maksab?
Man tai (ne)patinka.	Tas man (ne-)patīk.	Mulle see (ei) meeldi
gerai/blogai	labs/slikts	avatud/suletud
atidara/uždaryta	atvērts/slēgts	avatud/suletud
Labas rytas!/	Labrīt!/	Tere hommikust!/
Laba diena!	Labdien!	Tere päevast!/
Labas vakaras!/	Labvakar!/	Tere õhtust!/
Labanaktis!	Ar labu nakti!	Head ööd!
Sveiki!/Iki pasimatymo!	Sveiki!/Uz redzēšanos!	Tere!/Head aega!
Iki!	Atā!	Nägemist!
Mano vardas ...	Mani sauc ...	Minu nimi on ...
Koks tavo vardas?	Kā Jūs sauc?	Mis Teie nimi on?
geležinkelio stotis/uostas	Esmu no ...	Ma olen ...
išvykimo/atvykimo	(dzelzceļa) stacija/osta	raudtejaam/sadam
išvykimo/atvykimo	atiešana/pienākšana	ärasõit/saabumine
Kuri valanda?	Cik (ir) pulkstenis?	Mis kell on?
Dabar trys valandos.	Pulkstenis ir trīs.	Kell on kolm.
šiandien/rytoj/	šodien/rīt/	täna/homme/
vakar	vakar	eile
Prašom, valgiaraštį!	Lūdzu, atnesiet ēdienkarti!	Menüüd, palun.
Aš norēčiau ...?	Vai varu palūgt ...?	Ma tahan, palun, ...?
peilis/šakutė/šaukštelis	nazis/dakša/karote	nuga/kahvel/lusikas
druska/pipirai/cukrus	sāls/pipari/cukurs	sool/pipar/suhkur
actas/aliejus	etiķis/eļļa	äädikas/õli
pienas/grietinėlė	piens/saldais krējums	milk/koor
su/be ledo	ar ledu / bez ledus	jääga/ilma jääta
vegetariškas	veģetārietis/veģetāriete	taimetoitlane
Prašom, sąskaitą!	Es vēlos samaksāt.	Palun, arvet!

USEFUL PHRASES

ENGLISH	RUSSIAN	FINNISH
IN BRIEF		
yes/no/maybe	dá/nét/mózhet byt	kyllä/ei/ehkä
please/thank you	pozhálusta/spasibo	ole hyvä/kiitos
Sorry!	Izwiní	Anteeksi!
Excuse me!	Izwinítje!	Anteeksi!
May I ...?	Mózhno?	Saanko ...?
Pardon?	Proshú proschtschéniya?	Anteeksi, kuinka?
I would like to ...	ja chatschú ...	Haluaisin ...
Have you got ...?	U wás jést ...?	Onko teillä ...?
How much is ...?	Skólko stóit ...?	Kuinka paljon maksaa ...?
I (don't) like this.	Eto mnje (ne) nráwica.	Pidän siitä./En pidä siitä.
good/bad	horoschó/plócho	hyvä/huono
open/closed	otkrýto/zakrýto	auki/suljettu
SALUTATION & TRAVEL		
Good morning!/	dóbraje útra!/	Hyvää huomenta!/
afternoon!	dóbry djen!	päivää!
Good evening!/	Dóbryj wétscher!/	Hyvää iltaa!
night!	Spokójnoj nótschi!	Hyvää yötä!
Hello!/Goodbye!	Priwét/Do swidánija!	Hei! /Näkemiin!
Bye!	Poká!	Heippa!
My name is ...	Menjá sowút ...	Minun nimeni on ...
What's your name?	Kak was sowút?	Mitä teidän nimenne on?
I'm from ...	Ya iz ...	Minä olen ...
station/harbour	woksál/port	rautatieasema/satama
departure/arrival	otjézd/pribýtije	lähtevät (junat)/saapuvat
What time is it?	Kotóryj tschás?	Mitä kello on?
It's three o'clock.	Seytschás tri tschasá.	Kello on kolme.
today/tomorrow/	segódnja/záwtra/	tänään/huomenna/
yesterday	wtscherá	eilen
FOOD & DRINK		
The menue, please.	Menjú pozhálusta.	Saisinko ruokalistan.
May I have ...?	Wy ne prinesjóte	Saisinko ...?
	mne ...?	
knife/fork/spoon	nozh/vílka/lózhka	veitsi/haarukka/lusikka
salt/pepper/sugar	sol'/pérets/sákhar	suola/pippuri/sokeri
vinegar/oil	úksus/rastítel'noje máslo	etikka/öljy
milk/cream	molokó/slíwki	maito/kerma
with/without ice	so l'dom/bez bez l'da	jäillä/ilman jäitä
vegetarian	wegetarianéz	kasvissyöjä
May I have the bill,	Ja hotschý zaplatít.	Lasku, olkaa hyvää.
please?		

Short and sweet

This short list of phrases will help you say the most important words and phrases in the languages listed below:

SWEDISH	DANISH
ja/nej/kanske	ja/nej/måske
Varsågod./Tack.	værsgod/tak
Ursäkta./	Undskyld!
Förlåt.	Undskyld!
Får jag...?	Må jeg ...?
Ursäkta?	Undskyld?/Hvad?
Jag skulle gärna vilja ...	Jeg vil gerne ...
Har du ...?	Har du ...?
Hur mycket kostar ...?	Hvad koster ...?
Det tycker jag (inte) om.	Det kan jeg (ikke) lide.
bra/dåligt	godt/dårligt
öppet/stängt	åben/lukket
God morgon!/	God morgen!/
Hej!	dag!
Godkväll!	God aften!
God natt!	God nat!
Hej!/Hej då	Hej!/Farvel!
Hej då!	Hej hej!
Jag heter ...	Jeg hedder ...
Vad heter du?	Hvad hedder De?
Jag kommer från ...	Jeg kommer fra ...
centralstationen/hamnen	station/havn
avgång/ankomst	afgang/ankomst
Vad är klockan?	Hvad er klokken?
Klockan är tre.	Klokken er tre.
idag/i morgon/	idag/imorgen/
igår	igår
Menyn, tack.	Spisekortet, tak.
Skulle jag kunna få ...?	Jeg vil gerne have ...
kniv/gaffel/sked	kniv/gaffel/ske
salt/peppar/socker	salt/peber/sukker
Ättika/olja	eddike/olie
Mjölk/grädde	mælk/fløde
med/utan is	med/uden is
Vegetarian	vegetar
Jag skulle gärna vilja betala, tack.	Jeg vil gerne betale.

HOW TO CRUISE

EMBARKING

On arrival at the cruise terminal, you hand over your baggage. Remember to put important items you will need after you have gone aboard in your hand luggage, as it may take quite a while before the suitcases are brought to the relevant cabins. At the check-in point you will get your boarding pass and a security check. If you are lucky, you can go on board immediately, but it is also possible that you may have to stay in the waiting hall a little longer before it's your turn.

DISEMBARKING

Put your bags outside the cabin door the evening before disembarking. Once again: Keep anything you will need the next morning with your hand luggage.

EMERGENCY DRILL

All passengers must take part in the emergency drill, which usually takes place on the day of embarkation. You will find a life jacket in your cabin which you must put on for the drill. You will be informed of the drill on the PA system; proceed to your allocated master station, which is a place near the lifeboats. This is where the actual practice is done.

LIFEBOATS

The number of lifeboats is prescribed by international law and exceeds the maximum passenger capacity by 125 per cent.

Finally on board!

Tips & tricks for your cruise

Is this your first big cruise? We have collected some info and concepts for you about life on the high seas.

"Women and children first" does not apply to emergencies; for handicapped persons there are boats adapted to their special needs.

MEDICAL CARE

Cruise ships have medical personnel on board; on the larger ships, there is even a hospital. Any serious case of sickness is transferred to a hospital on land. Find out to what extent your medical insurance covers any medical treatment for which you initially have to pay yourself. In case of doubt, take out appropriate international health insurance.

SEASICKNESS

On the Atlantic, the weather can sometimes change and turn stormy, which will make the going a bit rougher. The stabilisers of modern ships suppress most of the rolling, but in severe cases they cannot completely eliminate it. To be on the safe side, you can buy medication against seasickness at a pharmacy.

BERTHING TIMES

Before going ashore, you will be informed how much time you have available. You must show your boarding pass when leaving and returning to the ship. Note: Allow enough time for your return to the ship. Even though ships wait a while for delayed passengers, sooner or later they have to leave, as extended stays in port incur costs for the shipping line. Once it has left, you've got a problem.

The gangway leads into the ship

SHORE EXCURSIONS

You can book shore excursions, including shuttle buses, on board and join sightseeing trips, for example. But you can also organise your on-shore activities yourself. If you want to go off on our own, you will find taxis in most ports; sometimes you're lucky and can reach the city centre on foot.

ROADSTEAD

Many ports are too small for large cruise ships to enter. In such cases the ships anchor outside; they ride at anchor "in the roadstead".

TENDER BOAT

Passengers are carried ashore from ships lying in a roadstead by smaller boats, called tenders or tender boats, for their excursions.

DRESS

Although dress rules have become less strict nowadays because of the greater variety of cruise ships, you should enquire what dress code is required on board your ship. As a general rule: The more stars a ship has, the more formal the dress. The dress code for dinner is usually indicated on the board programme for the day. Many shipping lines publish the dress rules on their website.

TIPPING

Many cruise lines charge a flat rate at the end of the trip that is allocated to the crew. Other lines leave it up to you how much you want to tip whom. If uncertain, enquire at your line what their customs are.

ICEBREAKERS

Cruises are also very popular with people travelling alone. For these passengers the lines arrange appropriate evenings where one can get to know other passengers travelling alone. Don't worry, these evenings are not dating occasions!

ON-BOARD ACCOUNT

All purchases made on board are cashless transactions. When you embark, you register your credit card or pay a deposit. Dollars and euros are the most common cruise currencies. Note that in the case of dollars, conversion fees are charged to the credit card account. You receive your cruise account before you disembark. What you pay afterwards is charged separately.

ON-BOARD PROGRAM AND BUSINESS

On cruise ships, entertainment is provided at appropriate (evening) events. Shops and boutiques are provided for shopping.

CABIN INFORMATION

On cruise ships, there are normally four classes of cabins that differ quite a bit as regards furnishings and price.

▶ **Inside cabins:** These are the cheapest type, without a view of the sea and with rather limited space.

▶ **Outside cabins:** Here the porthole allows you to see the sea, but the cabins are usually not noticeably larger than inside cabins.

▶ **Balcony cabins:** These have their own balcony, which can be an advantage if the weather is fine.

▶ **Suites:** the most expensive category, with better furnishings, more space and additional service.

ABC OF SHIPPING

Aft – rear part of the ship (stern, poop)

Anchor – keeps the ship in place; cruise ships have several

Bearing – direction of travel of a ship, course

Bell(s) – nautical indication of time in half hours

Bow – front part of a ship

Bridge – place from where the captain steers the ship

Bunker – fuel store (tanks) on a ship

Captain – person in command of a ship

Companionway – narrow stairway inside a ship

Dock – part of a port where a ship moors

Fathom – nautical measure of length; a fathom equals six feet

Flagship – best ship of a shipping line, often also the largest and newest

Galley – ship's kitchen

Gangway – stair or bridge whereby the passengers embark

Heave to – slowing down and changing direction of a ship

Hull – body of a ship, without superstructure

Keel – part of a ship running continuously from stem to stern of a ship and mostly submerged

Knot – nautical unit of speed; 1 knot = 1 nautical mile per hour

Lee – the downwind side of a ship

Luff – the upwind (windward) side of a ship

Maiden voyage – first voyage of a ship with passengers

Master stations – waiting areas at the lifeboats in emergencies

Mayday – international call for help on sea

Nautical mile – nautical unit of measurement, equal to 1852 m / 1.1508 mi

Pier – mooring place for ships (also called a quay)

Pilot – steers the ship through tricky waters

Pitching – Lengthwise up-and-down movement of a ship

Port fee – is calculated in each port on the basis of a ship's size

Porthole – round window

Port side – left side of a ship (looking forward)

Purser – ship's officer who keeps the accounts

Rolling – lateral swinging of a ship

Set sail – to depart from a port on a course

Sextant – nautical measuring instrument for determining position

Sister ships – ships with the same construction and belonging to the same line

SOS – international distress code

Starboard side – right-hand side of a ship (looking forward)

Stern – rear part of the ship *(see* Aft)

Swell – movement of water caused by wind

Tide – daily rise and fall of the sea level (ebb and flow)

Wake – water trail dragged along by a ship while sailing

Watch – on-duty time of the crew

Waterline – height of the water level measured on the ship's hull

Weighing anchor – raising the anchor before the ship sails

Yawing – not steering a straight course

INDEX

This index lists selected places of interest and worth seeing that are mentioned in this tour guide.

INDEX

PICTURE CREDITS

Cover: Copenhagen (© fotolia.com/Horváth Botond);
Photos: Horváth Botond (1); © fotolia.com: Yevgen Belich (4), ©Gabriele Rohde – stock.adobe.com (6/7), patti-labelle – stock.adobe.com (8/9), Madlen Steiner – stock.adobe.com (12), Gabriele Rohde (14/15, 2 bottom), Bri-gitte Bohnhorst (16), ©powell83 – stock.adobe.com (19), powell83 (20), Claus Schlüter (22), ©Marc Heiligen-stein – stock.adobe.com (23), peno – penofoto.de (25), Fotolyse (26), ©Bertold Werkmann – stock.adobe.com (28), ©M.Franke - stock.adobe.com (29), pure-life-pictures (31, 2 top), Wolfgang Jargstorff (32), Rico Ködder (35), pure-life-pictures (36), autofocus67 (39), JackF (42/43), Roman Babakin (45), pixs:sell (46), ©elenarostunova – stock.adobe.com (47), Mike Mareen (49), Justyna Kaminska – stock.adobe.com (50), ©mindelio – stock.ado-be.com (52/53), Darius Dzinnik (54), ©thauwald-pictures – stock.adobe.com (55), ©proslgn – stock.adobe.com (56), chamillew (58/59), bortnikau (60), ronstik (61), Oleg Mitiukhin (63), liramaigums (64), ronstik (65), Sean-PavonePhoto (66/67), Mikhail Markovskiy (69), globetrotter1 (70), f11photo (72/73), Dmitri Maruta (74), vladimir (75), pankow (77), ©Jacek - stock.adobe.com (78), ©nblxer - stock.adobe.com (80/81), Oleksiy Mark (83), ©Paul - stock.adobe.com (84), ©visualpower – stock.adobe.com (85), ©Martin – stock.adobe.com (86), ©Marco2811 – stock.adobe.com (88), ©tl6781 – stock.adobe.com (90/91, 3 bottom), ©pure-life-pictures – stock.adobe.com (93), ©dudlajzov – stock.adobe.com (94), ©Thierry GUIMBERT – stock.adobe.com (96), ©dimbar76 – stock.ado-be.com (97), ©Charlotte – stock.adobe.com (99), Vien Hoang (100), ©weixx – stock.adobe.com (103), Adam Höglund (104), ©norikko – stock.adobe.com (105), ©rolf_52 – stock.adobe.com (106), ©cmfotoworks – stock.adobe.com (108/109, 3 top), ©boysen – stock.adobe.com (110), Maridav (114), ©anshar73 – stock.adobe.com (115), ©hwtravel – stock.adobe.com (116), ©visualpower – stock.adobe.com (118), ©cmfotoworks – stock.adobe.com (119), ©yegorov_nick – stock.adobe.com (121), ©thomaslerchphoto – stock.adobe.com (122); © mauritius Images: Catharina Lux / (10/11), Johannes Pistorius (113), Juan SiLVA/Alamy (128), Jochen Tack/Alamy (129); © iStock.com: mikdam (05), apomares (130)

WRITE TO US

e-mail: info@marcopologuides.co.uk

Did you have a great holiday? Is there something on your mind? Whatever it is, let us know! Whether you want to praise, alert us to errors or give us a personal tip – MARCO POLO would be pleased to hear from you.
We do everything we can to provide the very latest information for your trip. Nevertheless, despite all of our authors' thorough research, errors can creep in. MARCO POLO does not accept any liability for this. Please contact us by e-mail or post.

MARCO POLO Travel Publishing Ltd
Pinewood, Chineham Business Park
Crockford Lane, Chineham
Basingstoke, Hampshire RG24 8AL
United Kingdom

1st edition 2020
Worldwide Distribution: Marco Polo Travel Publishing Ltd, Pinewood, Chineham Business Park, Crockford Lane, Basingstoke, Hampshire RG24 8AL, United Kingdom. Email: sales@marcopolouk.com
© MAIRDUMONT GmbH & Co. KG, Ostfildern
Chief editor: Stefanie Penck
Authors: Klaus Bötig, Dorothea Heintze, Silvia Propp, Anke Lübbert, Marc Engelhardt, Thoralf Plath, Katarzyna Tuszyńska, Jan Pallokat, Birgit Johannsmeier, Lothar Deeg, Joseann Freyer-Lindner, Clemens Bomsdorf, Tatjana Reiff, Carina Tietz, Thomas Eckert; Coauthors: Katrin Wienefeld, Izabella Gawin, Majke Gerke, Sabine Spatzek, Thoralf Plath, Bruno Kaufmann, Karin Bock-Häggmark, Christoph Schumann, Carina Tietz
Cartography and pull-out maps: © MAIRDUMONT, Ostfildern
Translated from German by Clarien Kurzepa, Jane Riester, Robert McInnes, Suzanne Kirkbright, Tony Halliday
Pre-press: trans texas publishing services GmbH, Cologne

All rights reserved. No part of this book may be reproduced, stored in a retrieval system or transmitted in any form or by any means (electronic, mechanical, photocopying, recording or otherwise) without prior written permission from the publisher.

Printed in China

MIX
Paper from responsible sources
FSC® C124385

DOS AND DON'TS ☝

Details you should know

OFFENDING RELIGIOUS FEELINGS

You will encounter Russian Orthodox churches in many places in the Baltics, and they are almost always open for sightseeing, which is worthwhile because of the magnificent decor and age-old icons. But they are places of worship, the strict religiosity is genuine and not folklore. Remember this when you enter an orthodox church! Please do not go in sexy leisure clothes, and be sensitive with the camera. The same applies in the Catholic churches of Lithuania and Poland.

BEING IMPATIENT

Finns wait patiently until it is their turn. And that also applies to Sweden. Here there is no pushing and shoving, one should be well-behaved in a queue. If possible, with enough space between you and the next person.

IT MIGHT ALL LOOK LIKE AMBER

Yellow-brown pebbles or polished brown glass shards often look like amber. Whether your beach find is really amber, you'll quickly find out with the rub test: when a larger piece of amber is rubbed against fabric, unlike pebbles or glass, it becomes electrostatically charged and attracts scraps of paper. With small pieces, the test is usually unsuccessful, in which case you should dissolve two tablespoons of table salt in a glass of water. Amber floats because of its low density, whereas pebbles and glass sink to the ground.

TAKING PHOTOS OF EVERYTHING

It is understandable that there is a wish to banish the capturing of many travel memories in the form of photos and videos: be considerate and obtain consent before you photograph people. A friendly smile often works wonders! And accept a no.

BEING ROBBED

Wherever many people are bustled together, there will also always be some shady characters to reckon with. Take good care of your valuables, especially in big cities; when strolling through the city, the handbag and the camera are always worn on the side facing the wall. Chest and waist bags are the safest.

TOO CLOSE TO MILITARY OBJECTS

Filming and photographing military objects in Poland, is strictly forbidden, even as a NATO member, Poland's military is allergic to extremely obvious interest in its facilities. On the Polish coast there are two large military restricted areas.